巡闢齋

首陽吉金

胡盈瑩 范季融藏中國古代青銅器

ANCIENT CHINESE BRONZES
FROM THE SHOUYANG STUDIO
The Katherine and George Fan Collection

首陽齋 · 上海博物館 · 香港中文大學文物館

Shouyang Studio · Shanghai Museum
Art Museum, The Chinese University of Hong Kong

上海展覽得到了瑞士信貸銀行的大力支持，謹致謝忱。
The exhibition in Shanghai has been supported by a grant from Credit Suisse.

展覽策劃：范季融　陳爕君　李朝遠　陳克倫　林業強
Exhibition management:
George Fan, Chen Xiejun, Li Chaoyuan, Chen Kelun, Peter Lam

·

展覽協調：周　亞　李仲謀
Exhibition coordination: Zhou Ya, Li Zhongmou

·

上海展覽設計：李蓉蓉　張莉娟
Exhibition design (Shanghai): Li Rongrong, Zhang Lijuan

·

香港展覽設計：寧雄斌　梁超權
Exhibition design (Hong Kong): Gary Ning, Eric Leung

·

圖錄：首陽齋　上海博物館　香港中文大學文物館合編
Catalogue jointly edited by Shouyang Studio, Shanghai Museum and Art Museum, The Chinese University of Hong Kong

·

展品著錄：周　亞　馬今洪　胡嘉麟
Catalogue entries: Zhou Ya, Ma Jinhong, Hu Jialin

·

英文翻譯：李仲謀　陸鵬亮　王　佳　金靖之
English Translation: Li Zhongmou, Lu Pengliang, Wang Jia, Jin Jingzhi

·

英文審校：林業強　陳娟安
English editing: Peter Lam, Kellyon Chan

·

攝影：汪雯梅
Photography: Wang Wenmei

·

拓片：謝海元
Rubbings: Xie Haiyuan

·

繪圖：周根寶
Line drawings: Zhou Genbao

·

目 錄 CONTENTS

序 言

　　青銅器是中國古代文化藝術品中的傑出代表。地處美國紐約的首陽齋多年來珍藏有百餘件中國古代青銅文物，被視爲當今世界該藝術門類的重要私人收藏之一。

　　"首陽齋"是上海博物館捐贈人、美國著名華裔收藏家胡盈瑩、范季融伉儷的齋名。齋主十分注重青銅器所蘊涵的文化與學術內涵，把收藏青銅器看作是一個學習和研究中國傳統文化的過程，在海外收藏家中獨樹一幟。

　　本次展覽精選首陽齋所藏七十件（組）青銅文物，涵蓋了我國青銅工藝發展過程中各時期的作品，並包含諸多帶有銘文的器物，具有珍貴的學術研究和藝術鑒賞價值。

　　首陽齋所藏青銅器迄今爲止從未公開展出過。此次上海博物館與其合作舉辦展覽，定將彌補國內公私收藏之不足，對於國內學者進一步瞭解和研究海外所藏中國古代青銅文物具有重要意義。

上海博物館館長

陈燮君

PREFACE

Bronzes are true monuments of the history of arts in China's antiquity. The Shouyang Studio collection in New York, USA of over one hundred pieces of ancient Chinese bronze assembled over the years is a world-class private collection of its kind.

'Shouyang Studio' is the private hall name of Dr. and Mrs. George Fan, who are well-known Chinese American collectors, as well as generous benefactors to the Shanghai Museum. They fully recognize the role and importance of bronzes in the study of the culture and heritage of China. Hence they always reckon that collecting bronzes should be an academic process. Their insight is remarkable among oversea collectors.

This exhibition displays seventy pieces/sets of bronze wares selected from the Shouyang Studio collection to illustrate milestones in the development of bronze art and technology in China. The selection includes quite a number of pieces with inscriptions that provide a wealth of information for academic study in addition to the aesthetic value.

The bronze collection of the Shouyang Studio has never been featured in any exhibitions before. It is with pleasure that the Shanghai Museum mounts this exhibition in collaboration with Dr. and Mrs. George Fan. The exhibition provides a rare opportunity for bronze scholars from the Mainland to have a fuller picture of the quality, characteristics and other aspects of Chinese bronzes in overseas collections.

Chen Xiejun
Director, Shanghai Museum

蒐藏青銅器

范季融

多年前在機緣巧合下，曾經協助馬承源館長爲上海博物館入藏西周冒鼎。自始之後，激發起我對蒐藏青銅器的興趣。馬先生不厭其詳地爲我解釋冒鼎的資料，其錯綜複雜的歷史及文化背景，引人入勝。一直醉心中國歷史文化的我，對中國文化肇始階段的青銅時代興趣濃厚。研習這階段歷史的有效方法，是透過同時代的實物去學習，如此會更加具體和易於掌握。大部分收藏家都單純以美學角度去鑒賞青銅器，我一開始已非如此，我對理性分析當時的時代背景更感興趣。由於我首要的目標是對青銅時代的歷史和文化有更深刻的瞭解，因此我的收藏路向也和其他藏家有別。以器物爲本的研究方法，使我對青銅時代中各個不同階段有更全面的瞭解，亦對河南安陽以外的其他區域有更多的認識。安陽是晚商時期的都城，西方青銅器收藏家的注意力大多集中於此。透過對特定器物及相關資料進行研究，我對當時的青銅器稍有所領悟。

一件器物是歷史的客觀體現，但是首要條件是該器物必須是真實無訛的。所以，爲了實現目標，先決條件便是學習如何鑒別青銅器的真僞。除了參閱文獻資料外，我多次親赴上海研習。馬承源館長是我的良師，他向我展示了上海博物館所藏的大批珍貴青銅器，詳細講解有關器物的風格、鑄造方法和器表銹蝕狀況等。講授內容有異於課堂式的系統授課，馬先生以實物爲例，與我分享他積累多年的淵博知識，這是難能可貴的學習機會。在授課過程中，有時他會摻雜一些晚期甚至後仿器物，以測試我能否正確識辨。陳佩芬女士亦經常參與，她也是我的良師益友。

我在當時，甚至直到現在所關注的一些課題包括：

1.中國青銅器的肇始；

2.不同類型的青銅器及其用途；

3.青銅器在中國悠久的青銅時代中的發展；

4.青銅時代在中國文化形成過程中的作用和地位。

前三者，促使我蒐集早期不同類型的青銅器。青銅器的器形及鑄造方法雖然不是我關注的重點，但却讓我瞭解到青銅鑄造業的發達及其地域性文化的發展。青銅時代歷時約兩千年，年代跨度長，部分青銅器經歷了一至兩代的風格轉變。最後一個課題正是我的興趣核心所在，像我這樣一個接受西方科學技術教育的人，中國文化自始至終都不是我的知識重點。在學習青銅時代文化的過程中，我感到十分驚嘆，因爲今天的中國文化，大多植根於三千多年前青銅時代先王們的歷史、教育和哲學思維等，而且我們的思想和日常生活至今仍深受這些古文化影響。

自宋代以來，金石學者鑽研青銅器銘文，這些銘文除了是古文字學的研究內容之外，還可以證史，有重要的史料價值。要運用銘文來證史，必先熟悉歷史典籍、記載和古文獻。作爲一個門外漢，我並無這方面的基本訓練，因此必須別覓蹊徑。我先花時間識讀青銅器銘刻內容，然後尋找任何與之相關的史料、文獻和史事記載，嘗試從中找到一些可識別的人名或一些與紀年史事有關連的細節。很幸運，首陽齋的部分藏品正提供了一些與著名歷史人物和歷史事件有關的資料。青銅器鑄刻銘文所載，雖然都是史實，但很多銘文中的人、地、事、物，往往不見載於歷史文獻，而且大部分銘文都很簡略，所以必須更深更廣地蒐尋相關的史料，翻閱枯燥乏味的歷史文獻，始能描繪出銘文的歷史圖像，重現當時的歷史背景。縱然這樣的學習過程要靠點滴積累、並非很有系統，但却能使我對當時的史事有更深刻和更全面的瞭解。回首過去，儘管這是鑽研中國歷史的另類方法，但對我而言，却是行之有效的。例如，在研究舌簋的過程中，我學到有關諸侯的事迹及其對中國文化的影響。而通過瞭解秦國的青銅器，也讓我得知商鞅對秦國崛起所作的貢獻，並最終促成六國的統一。這樣的例子繁多，不勝枚舉。

在蒐藏的初期，我對應該用怎樣的美學準則來鑒賞以及蒐集青銅器，曾經有過一番挣扎。我對中國陶瓷器的收藏，稍有認識；但是，鑒賞陶瓷和銅器這兩門藝術形式的準則，截然不同。出色的設計、釉色和器形都是鑒賞陶瓷和斷代的重要標準，所以我們收藏陶瓷時，要求精、真、新，通常會擯棄一些有瑕疵缺陷的器物。我們鑒賞陶瓷的眼光，就正如多個世紀前的陶工和鑒藏家一樣。我們會對宋代陶人素雅的品位、清代唐英督燒御窰器的高超技藝，或者宮廷造辦處工匠的精美琺瑯彩推崇備至。我認爲這是鑒賞藝術的普遍方式，觀者除了欣賞文物之美外，同時也會探究製作該器物的工匠和藝人。青銅器則提供一個不同的視野，出土的青銅器很多需要清洗和修復，現在每件銅器的色澤和表面的銹蝕，均與當年鑄造工匠和器物主人所見的有所不同。遺留至今的有些青銅重器，已經嚴重銹蝕破損，因此不管我們所見的器物如何完整、美觀，這只是重新修復的結果。事實上，爲我修復藏品的技師，經常問我清洗銅器需要到甚麼程度？我也曾經收到一些被藏家或古董商過分清洗的青銅器。往往，在一大批青銅器前，我經常問自己：這些器物看上去十分美觀，但它原來是否真的如此？在這種情況下，收藏家要做出最後的仲裁，決定文物應該清洗修復至甚麼程度。這點對衆多的青銅器專家可能不是甚麼問題，但這煩惱一直困擾着我，也只好自行尋求答案。

假若沒有我的良師益友——已故的上海博物館館長馬承源先生的個人指導，我對青銅器會一無所知，也不會引起我對青銅器的熱忱。我的摯友及顧問李朝遠博士於2007年來紐約首陽齋挑選展品，並誠邀到上海博物館展出。張光裕博士多次和我結伴走訪古董商和拍賣行，相互之間的討論讓我獲益匪淺。衷心感謝上海博物館青銅部的專家學者們，自我開始蒐藏青銅器至今，他們在周亞先生的領導下，爲拙藏進行化驗、清洗及修復工作，並在展覽的不同層面上提供具體幫助。最後感謝香港中文大學文物館林業強館長及該館同人，協助展覽圖錄的出版事宜，並安排展覽運至香港展出。對以上各合作單位的積極協助和用心付出，本人不勝感激。

Collecting Bronzes

George Fan

My interest in Chinese bronze was sparked after accidentally helping Mr. Ma Chengyuan to obtain a Western Zhou inscribed tripod, the Juan Ding for the Shanghai Museum. When Mr. Ma meticulously explained to me later on about that piece, I was fascinated by the intricate history and culture context. I have long been interested in learning more about Chinese culture and history, especially of the Bronze Age, the time when Chinese culture was formed. Looking for an effective way to study the era, I thought that studying actual artifacts of the time would be a more concrete and tractable approach. From the start I actually did not look at Chinese bronze from a purely aesthetical point of view, which is the main motivation for most collectors, but was more interested in the intellectual context. Since my prime target is to gain some understanding about the culture and history of the Bronze Age, my course of collection took a different route from others. The object-oriented tours took me to all different periods within the Bronze Age and also took me through different regions of China far away from the metropolitan Anyang, the late Shang capital where Western collectors at large have been focused upon. By doing research on selected pieces and some related items, I did gain some insights of the era, however limited it might be.

An artifact is the embodiment of history, provided that it is a genuine piece. Hence, learning the complicated process of authentication of bronzes is a prerequisite for achieving my goals. Besides learning to authenticate artifacts by reading published texts and materials, I made many study trips to Shanghai. My teacher was Director Ma Chengyuan, who showed me good examples from the extensive museum collection and lectured me on styles, construction methods and surface conditions. The teaching was rather unstructured, but he was so generous in sharing his vast knowledge. It was an unusual learning opportunity. In some sessions he mixed some later pieces with the genuine ones to test if I could identify and differentiate them. Ms. Chen Peifen often joined us as the co-teacher.

Some of the issues that interested me at that time, and even now, are:
1. The inception of Chinese bronze
2. Different types of bronzes and their usages
3. The evolution of bronzes in the long-lasting Bronze Age in China
4. The role of the Bronze Age in the formation of Chinese culture

The first three aspects drove me to search for early bronzes as well as the varied forms of bronzes. And then, bronze shapes and casting methods, though not my principal concern, have taught me the dynamics of the industry and the regional cultures. We saw in the objects that in the long span of the Bronze Age, some 2000 years, they went through the stylistic changes in one generation or two. The final issue in no time became the core area of my interest. For a person who has received Western education in science and technology like me, Chinese culture has never been a central part of the knowledge to be acquired. By studying the culture of the Bronze Age I was amazed to learn that so much of present-day Chinese culture is rooted in the history, teaching, thoughts and philosophy of the princes and kings of the Bronze Age some three millennia ago. Our thoughts and day-to-day life are still strongly influenced by this ancient culture.

Scholars have long since believed that the value of inscription is to attest and verify the documented history. To do that, they are, first of all, well familiar with the written history and many ancient texts. My study did not follow this path because as an outsider I had no such training. I used information from inscribed bronzes to search whatever might be related and available in the documented history. It was particularly rewarding if a named person could be identified or the details could be traced to a chronicled historical event. I am very fortunate to have some pieces that provide information related to well-known historical figures and events. As a matter of fact, many of the principals in the inscriptions are unrecorded in the written documents.

Because of the brevity of most inscriptions I had to search far and wide through, in my opinion, very dry historical texts. As I waded through numerous passages, a picture of events of the period was established and Chinese history became alive for me. Although such a learning process was spotty, I went into great detail about the activities of certain periods. Looking back, that was a very strange way to learn history, notwithstanding, I found it workable. For instance, by studying the She *gui* I learned about the events with relation to the grand duke and his influence on Chinese culture. By reading up on Qin bronzes I learned about Shang Yang and his contribution to the rise of the Qin State, which led to the unification of China. There are many examples, too numerous to be all mentioned here.

I had a difficult time in esthetic issues of bronzes from the very beginning. Prior to studying bronzes I was a student of Chinese ceramics. The rules of looking at these two art forms are very different. In ceramics we usually reject items with defects since the appreciation of the remarkable design, colour and shape of the object is quintessential. We see the ceramics as the potters or the connoisseurs saw them many centuries ago when they were first fired. Through these *objets d'art* we admire the elegant taste of Song potters, the technical perfection of the Qing imperial kiln supervisors such as Tang Ying or the fine paintings in enamel by the artists of the Court academy. I think this is a rather common way of looking at art in general, the viewer besides appreciating the beauty of the object also try to find out who the artist was. Bronzes offer a different perspective. The excavated pieces need to be cleaned and very often to be repaired. In every case the patina and the surface condition are never the ones seen by the original bronze-smith or the owner. Some of the most well-known bronzes were heavily restored, so what we see are the newly altered forms, no matter how beautiful they are. In fact I was often asked by the restorers who cleaned bronzes for me to what extent the work should be done. I have also gotten pieces that the previous owners had them over-cleaned. Often I find myself standing in front of a great bronze asking the question: it looks wonderful but should it really look this way? In such a case, the collector plays the role of an arbiter in deciding what the 'artifact' should look like. While this fact does not seem to bother most bronze experts, I have yet to resolve this issue for myself.

The study would never have been possible without the personal guidance of my late mentor and good friend, Director Ma Chengyuan. Dr. Li Chaoyuan, a close friend and adviser in recent years, invited me to put up this show at the Shanghai Museum and made a selection during a visit to New York in 2007. Dr. Alex K.Y. Cheung has been a constant adviser. We made countless trips to dealers and auction houses together. The discussion we had is a high point of my experience. My thanks also goes to the staff of the Bronze Department of the Shanghai Museum who have worked with me from the very first piece I collected. They help me in testing, cleaning and the repair work of my bronzes. Recently, under the leadership of Zhou Ya, they have provided much help in all aspects of this exhibition. I am also grateful to Peter Lam and his colleagues at the Art Museum, The Chinese University of Hong Kong for their contribution and help in the technical matters of the exhibition catalogue and for arranging to let the exhibition to travel to Hong Kong.

我與季融先生的金石緣

張光裕

一晃眼我與范季融先生相交，已整整一十八年。我們的認識是經由馬承源先生的介紹。馬先生當年爲了籌建上海博物館新館，經常往來於香港與上海，當時范先生在香港中文大學擔任工程學院院長，他受到馬先生的啓發，對青銅器産生了濃厚的興趣，我們便在相互切磋中，開展了多年來的情誼。

那時候我們都住在同一校區，范先生興致來時，便就近邀我一起去逛荷李活道古肆。遇到心儀的珍品，便一起商討研究，凡是有銘文且有學術價值的青銅器，我會毫不猶疑地請他務必考慮留下。如有特別精彩的精品，他常會説這應該是博物館的東西，便主動地讓給公家收藏。他就是這樣一位豁達無私的謙謙君子。這次展覽的藏品，大部分我都有幸率先目驗，而且每件器物的背後都有一個小故事。例如秦公鼎三器便是因爲秦兩詔橢升的發現而一起購藏；盨簋、盨觶和盨瓪是同一人所鑄器，但却分別在不同時地所得，文物的散聚就是這樣的奇妙。商鞅鈹是目前海内外僅有的一件屬於商鞅的鈹器，但難以置信，該器竟然是在"吃仙丹"的情況下入藏的，事實上這正是藏器主人的福緣；宴射刻紋畫像匜，入目之初，全器黝黑一片，但隱約中可見花紋浮動，當時我們相視作出會心微笑，范先生不假思索便毅然購下，現在已成了藏器中最精彩的藝術精品之一，由此正可印證他的過人識力。

我們都記得馬承源先生曾經强調，頂級的青銅器固然是一件至高無上的藝術品，但是如果具備銘文的話，更足以見證及顯示歷史和文化的價值與意義，因此范先生特別重視有銘青銅器的收藏。展品中的智簋和雁侯見工簋便體現了青銅器銘文的重要，前者因爲一個"加（嘉）"字的出現，爲解決金文中聚訟已久的"蔑"一辭提供了重要的證據，後者器銘八十二字，主要陳述西周時王命雁侯征伐"淮南夷"（一般金文只稱"南淮夷"）事，可以補充西周時期南征史事所未備。

這次展出的藏品，不少都是未曾見於著録的帶銘青銅器，而新材料的展示，同時也樹立了探討中國歷史文化的另一個標竿，其意義非凡自然不在話下，對學術的推動和影響肯定也是深遠的。

A Memorable Ancient Chinese Bronzes Collection Brought Together through Destiny and Mutual Affinity

Cheung Kwong Yue

Director Ma Chengyuan introduced me to Mr. George J.Y. Fan some eighteen years ago. At that time Mr. Ma was preparing for the establishment of the new Shanghai Museum, and he had to travel between Hong Kong and Shanghai quite frequently. Mr. Fan was then the Dean of the Faculty of Engineering of the Chinese University of Hong Kong and inspired by Mr. Ma, he developed a strong interest in bronze vessels. As a result, the long-lasting friendship between Mr. Fan and myself began to flourish through the discussions with him in this area of mutual interest.

As we worked at the same CUHK campus at that time, we often ventured out together to walk around antique shops in Hollywood Road, and his enthusiasm was so high, it also affected me. Whenever we found some vessels of interest, we would discuss and examine the items together; moreover, if there were any inscribed bronzes of high academic value, without hesitation, I would ask him to consider keeping them for his own collections. In contrast to some collectors, if he saw any truly special bronze vessels, his first thoughts were to try and get them to the public museums and encouraged public institutions to buy such items, rather than buy them himself.

For the collections in this exhibit, I have had the opportunity to examine many of the pieces, and there exists a story behind most of them linked to many serendipitous occasions. For instance, the discovery and purchase of a *tuo sheng* with inscriptions of two Qin imperial edicts, and the chance purchase three *ding* made for the Duke of Qin. After his acquisition of a *gui* by 奮 in New York unknowingly to me, I found a *zhi* for him and later a *gu* that were cast by the same person, 奮. It is amazing that such relics scattered over different countries is together again. Another example of this was that I was able to negotiate the acquisition for Mr. Fan of a *pi* made with supervision of Shang Yang. Upon our first witnessing a *yi* it looked black and unspectacular with some hovering patterns barely visible on its inner surface. On examining this object, he decided to have it; it turned out to be a very rare object. The vessel has now become one of star items among his collections.

Mr. Ma once emphasized that a bronze vessel was a great artifact in itself; furthermore if a bronze was inscribed, it could further verify and reveal aspects of Chinese culture. The collection also includes some inscribed bronzes. It is interesting to take note of bronze vessels *gui* made for Hu and another *gui* made for the Marquis of Ying. The character *jia* '加' found on the former has provided important evidence for the disputed issue of the explanation of *mie-li* '蔑曆' across many bronze inscriptions. The latter has 82 characters inscribed on it, recounting the Duke of Ying's expedition of *Huai-nan yi* 淮南夷 during the Western Zhou (the event was usually only recorded as *Nan huai-yi* '南淮夷'); thus, the inscription explains and finishes the previously incomplete account of the southern expedition which took place in the Western Zhou period.

Most of the inscribed bronzes in the collection have not been previously published. Such new materials and sources information certainly would be helpful to academics in the study of the history and culture of China.

首陽齋藏金二三議

周　亞

范季融先生説他自小接受的是西方文化的教育，自從接觸中國古代青銅器以後，他感覺其中藴藏了豐富的中國古代文化和歷史知識。爲了能够從青銅器中學習中國的文化和歷史，他和夫人開始收藏中國古代的青銅器。他不僅注重有銘文青銅器的收藏，也儘可能地收集夏商周各個時期的青銅器，因而在他不算太多的青銅器收藏中，却能够基本涵蓋了中國古代青銅工藝發展過程中各個時期的青銅器。

此次胡盈瑩、范季融伉儷在其首陽齋收藏的中國古代青銅器中，精心挑選了70件（組）來上海博物館展出。在展覽的籌備過程中，我們得以對每件器物作仔細觀察，於是對這批青銅器有了一些認識。

一

早期青銅器因爲關係到中國青銅工藝的産生、青銅禮制的形成等問題的研究，一直被學術界所關注。雖然在甘肅、青海等地的馬家窑文化遺址、齊家文化遺址中出土有刀、錐、鑿、斧、鏡、飾件等青銅製品，但它們均爲單範澆鑄或鍛製而成。一般認爲只有用複合範製作的青銅容器出現，才意味着中國青銅工藝的真正産生。目前可以看到的比較完整的早期青銅容器，基本上都是二里頭文化遺址中出土的。二里頭文化現在一般被認爲屬於夏代晚期，這是中國青銅工藝真正的萌生發展時期，所以這一時期的每一件青銅器，對於瞭解當時的青銅工藝、研究中國青銅工藝的産生發展過程都是極其重要的實物資料。

根據2003年出版的《中國考古學·夏商卷》的統計，在當時已公佈的資料中，偃師二里頭遺址共出土青銅容器18件，其中青銅爵13件、青銅斝3件、青銅鼎1件、青銅盉1件。在其他二里頭文化遺址中也出土有少量的青銅容器，主要是爵、斝。此外在一些博物館也收藏有少量的二里頭時期青銅容器[1]。

在首陽齋藏金中就有一件形制特點和製作工藝都屬於二里頭文化時期的青銅爵。這件爵，窄流、寬短尾、束腰、平底、三錐足，口緣内側有一周凸邊，半環形鋬自口沿直至腹底，鋬上有鏤孔。足與腹底連接處有三角錐形凸出，這種現象與1980年河南洛寧出土的一件二里頭時期管流爵（或稱之爲角）相似[2]。在爵腹一側，有兩條隨器腹束放走向而設的凸起弧綫（圖一），這是我們在以往二里頭時期青銅爵上没有注意到的現象。它們是用作裝飾的綫條，還是爲加强器腹牢度所設，抑或是兩者的原因都有，這是一個值得關注的問題。

---

1. 中國社會科學院考古研究所《中國考古學·夏商卷》第109頁，中國社會科學出版社2003年版。
2. 中國青銅器全集編輯委員會《中國青銅器全集》（1）第11頁，文物出版社1996年版。

二里頭文化的青銅爵一般有兩種形式，一種製作較原始，具有較强的仿製當時陶爵的特點；另一種則較爲精緻，造型與綫條都表現出其自身的設計理念。根據考古資料和杜金鵬先生的統計和分類研究，前者一般出土於二里頭文化的第三期，後者則多數出土於二里頭文化的第四期[3]，兩者在時間上的更替，表明青銅工藝當時正迅速地發展和成熟。首陽齋所藏二里頭時期青銅爵的形制與1973年二里頭遺址三期文化中出土的一件青銅爵（ⅧT22③:6）非常接近，應該也是屬於二里頭文化三期的青銅製品。

圖一

與二里頭文化相連接的二里岡文化下層的青銅容器，關係到對夏商之際青銅工藝、青銅體制的沿承及發展變化的研究，自然也備受關注。但這一時期的青銅容器考古發現並不多見，據《鄭州商城》一書："二里岡下層二期是目前鄭州商城遺址二里岡各期中最早出土有青銅容器的一期，但所出土的青銅容器僅11件，器類也不多，只見斝、爵和盉三種"[4]。

首陽齋收藏的商代早期聯珠紋斝與《歐洲所藏中國青銅器遺珠》著録的聯珠紋斝非常相似，《歐洲所藏中國青銅器遺珠》作者認爲它屬於二里頭文化時期，但同時也指出"此器錐足較短，腹形更接近商代前期的斝，年代也可能稍晚一些"[5]。我們認爲首陽齋的這件斝整體形制上更接近於河南鄭州白家莊商代二里岡下層二期出土的青銅斝，斝頸部一側裝飾的空心聯珠紋，也是商代二里岡時期才開始在青銅器上運用得比較多的一種紋樣，二里頭文化時期青銅器上裝飾的一般都是實心聯珠紋。由此，我們認爲這件斝應該還是屬於二里岡下層文化時期，亦即商代早期的青銅器。值得注意的是，這件斝口沿上的三棱形釘狀柱的形式常見於二里頭文化遺址出土的青銅斝上，如二里頭遺址1984年發掘的M9中出土的斝[6]、1987年發掘的87TLVM1出土的斝[7]。這種柱的形式與二里岡時期青銅斝之柱的常見形式有別，從已知的考古資料來看，二里岡時期青銅斝之柱的形式已普遍采用了菌形方柱。這表明首陽齋收藏的這件斝，應該是處於二里頭文化與二里岡文化過渡時期的器物。如此，這件斝無疑又爲瞭解、研究二里岡下層文化時期的青銅器增加了一件實物資料，也爲探究青銅斝的形制在二里頭文化向二里岡文化發展、過渡時期的演變過程，提供了一件不可多得的實物資料。

二

首陽齋藏金中的筒形器也是我很感興趣的兩件青銅器，其中一組爲五件套，素面無紋飾，形制相同，大小依

3.杜金鵬《商周銅爵研究》，《考古學報》1994年第3期第263頁。

4.河南省文物考古研究所《鄭州商城》（中）第674頁，文物出版社2001年版。

5.李學勤、艾蘭《歐洲所藏中國青銅器遺珠》黑白圖版二、第311頁，文物出版社1995年版。

6.中國社會科學院考古研究所二里頭工作隊《1984年秋河南偃師二里頭遺址發現的幾座墓葬》，《考古》1986年第4期第318頁。

7.中國社會科學院考古研究所二里頭工作隊《河南偃師二里頭遺址發現新的銅器》，《考古》1991年第12期第1138頁。

次遞減，最大的一件有蓋，相互套裝後即成一件；另一件的形制相同，但在筒身處飾三道體軀交纏的兩頭龍紋。

　　這種形制的青銅器在考古資料中並不多見，在目前收集到的資料中有河北平山三汲出土一組五件套[8]、山東諸城藏家莊莒公孫潮子墓出土的兩件[9]、河南桐柏月河鄋子伯受墓中出土的一件（無蓋）[10]、河北滿城中山靖王劉勝墓出土一件[11]、廣西貴縣羅泊灣漢墓出土一件[12]、上海博物館收藏有一件。另外在林巳奈夫先生的《殷周時代青銅器之研究·殷周青銅器綜覽三》132頁之長壺類中也著錄有兩件筒形器，然未注明收藏者。除了上海博物館收藏的一件飾有絢紋和貝紋，以及劉勝墓出土一件通體飾菱形鳥紋外，其餘幾件均爲素面，諸城出土的兩件、上海博物館收藏的一件及林巳奈夫著錄的兩件在器腹兩側均有環耳。其中林巳奈夫先生著錄中“長壺3”不僅作鋪首銜環耳，而且在器腹下側設一個獸形鋬，有如商周時期罍形器上所設，器蓋設獸形鈕。

　　這種形制的筒形器，定名各不相同，平山筒形器的介紹文章直呼爲“杯”，諸城出土報告和貴縣出土報告中名爲“杯形壺”，桐柏出土報告中稱之爲“筒杯”，滿城出土報告作“盒”，林巳奈夫先生則定爲“長壺”。定名的不同表明對其用途認識的不同，杯是飲酒器，壺是容酒器。我們覺得對此類器物用途的認識，還必須從其形制特點等因素來考慮。我們將所知筒形器資料列表如下：

首陽齋藏1	最大的高14.8厘米	最大口徑5.6厘米	無環耳、蓋三環鈕	五件套
首陽齋藏2	高22.7厘米	口徑9厘米	無環耳、蓋三環鈕	
平山出土	最大的高15厘米	最大口徑5.8厘米	無環耳、蓋三環鈕	五件套
滿城漢墓	高14.5厘米	口徑5.5厘米	無環耳、環鈕	
桐柏出土	高17.7厘米	口徑9.3厘米	無環耳	失蓋
諸城出土	高32.9厘米	口徑11.5厘米	環耳，蓋三環鈕	
貴縣出土	高39.3厘米	口徑13.6厘米	環耳，蓋四環鈕	
上海博物館藏	高32厘米	口徑11.3厘米	鋪首銜環耳、蓋四鳥形鈕	
林著1	高32.4厘米		環耳，蓋四環鈕	
林著2	高43.4厘米		鋪首銜環耳，蓋四獸形鈕、獸形鋬	

　　根據列表可見，筒形器大致可分爲兩類，一類無環耳，一類有環耳。前者高度在14.5至22.7厘米之間，後者高度在32.4至43.4厘米之間。如果説前者的高度尚適宜於作飲酒器使用的話，後者的高度已無可能用作飲酒器使用。而且從現有青銅器資料來看，有蓋銅器絕大多數都是容器，很少用作飲酒器。

　　值得注意的是滿城中山靖王劉勝墓中還出土一套形制相同、大小依次遞減的鎏金菱形鳥紋杯（報告稱之爲橢圓形杯），根據《滿城漢墓發掘報告》中圖十六的“一號墓中室器物分佈圖”所標位置，它們與鎏金菱形鳥紋筒形器（報告稱之爲盒）是放置在一起的，表明它們之間存在組合關係。另外從紋飾及鎏金裝飾來看，它們之間也

8.劉昀華《青銅套杯和套鉢》，《文物春秋》1996年第1期第83頁。

9.山東諸城縣博物館《山東諸城臧家莊與葛布口村戰國墓》，《文物》1987年第12期第47頁。

10.南陽市文物研究所、桐柏縣文管辦《桐柏月河一號春秋墓發掘簡報》，《中原文物》1997年第4期第8頁。

11.中國社會科學院考古研究所、河北省文物管理處《滿城漢墓發掘報告》（上）第78頁，圖版三十九·3，文物出版社1980年版。

12.廣西壯族自治區博物館《廣西貴縣羅泊灣漢墓》第36頁，文物出版社1988年版。

圖二

應該存在組合關係。根據報告描述，五件鎏金菱形鳥紋杯的紋飾可分爲兩組，依器物由小到大排列，前三件飾一組圖案，後兩件飾另一組圖案，報告指出鎏金菱形紋筒形器的蓋、腹、底部則同時兼飾有這兩種圖案。在這一組合中杯爲飲酒器甚明，因此，我認爲筒形器不可能是飲酒器，當用作容酒器無疑。我們根據報告中鎏金菱形紋筒形器的外形尺寸，在減去推算出的蓋的高度後，計算出它的容量約爲200毫升。這個容量與報告所列鎏金菱形紋杯中第二件（1：4283）的容量爲196毫升是很接近的。依照存在五件一組筒形器的考古資料，我們推測完全有可能當時製作有五件容量與鎏金菱形鳥紋杯對等的鎏金菱形鳥紋筒形器，只是由於某種原因，其餘四件未被入葬而已。

劉昀華在介紹平山三汲出土五件套裝的筒形器時，也將其與平山三汲中山王墓出土的五件一組的套鉢作比較，雖然沒有明確指出它們之間存在組合關係，但也給與了我們足夠的提示和聯想。

既然筒形器不可能是飲酒器，只能是容酒器，那麼將其定名爲杯顯然是不對的。我們同時也認爲將其歸爲壺類器，定名爲"長壺"、"杯形壺"也是不準確的。縱觀商周時期所有的壺類器，都是小口、有頸、鼓腹、圈足的式樣，從金文"壺"字的常見字形也可得出相同的結論（圖二）。筒形器的器形均爲敞口，斜直腹下收，矮圈足，與壺類器的器形差距實在太大。我們認爲在尚未找到給此類器形定名的依據之前，將其稱之爲"筒形器"不失爲一種比較妥當的權宜之計。

首陽齋藏交龍紋筒形器之紋飾，多見於戰國中晚期青銅鼎上，甘肅平涼廟莊出土的鼎[13]、陝西咸陽塔兒坡出土中戠鼎和平鼎[14]、河南洛陽針織廠出土的Ⅱ式和Ⅳ式鼎[15]都裝飾有這種體軀交纏的兩頭龍紋。從鼎的器形來看，這幾件鼎都應該是東周王畿或三晉地區的器物。

上海博物館藏的筒形器（圖三），蓋設四個鳳鳥形鈕，蓋面飾兩道絢紋，中間飾一道貝紋。器口沿及器底各飾一道絢紋。器身飾三組由絢紋、貝紋組成的紋飾帶：上下各以一道絢紋作界欄，中間是三道貝紋。貝紋與絢紋，是三晉地區春秋戰國時期青銅器上流行的裝飾紋樣，侯馬鑄銅遺址出土有多塊絢紋範和貝紋範，但是像這樣以絢紋作界欄，間飾數道貝紋組成

圖三　（攝影／薛皓冰）

13.魏懷珩《甘肅平涼廟莊的兩座戰國墓》，《考古與文物》1982年第5期第27頁。

14.咸陽市博物館《陝西咸陽塔兒坡出土的銅器》，《文物》1975年第6期第69頁。

15.洛陽市文物工作隊《洛陽市針織廠東周墓（C1M5269）的清理》，《文物》2001年第12期第41頁。

大面積的主體裝飾並不多見（圖四）。

除了河南桐柏月河墓屬於春秋晚期、河北滿城漢墓及廣西貴縣羅泊灣漢墓屬於西漢早期外，其餘數件筒形器從器形、紋飾分析都屬於戰國時期，特別是戰國中晚期。根據僅有幾件筒形器的出土地點分析，其分布的地域除了羅泊灣漢墓地處西南，桐柏月河墓屬於楚文化區域外，其餘的幾件應該都屬於中原地區的器物。

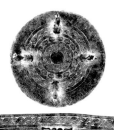

三

經過長時間無數學人的研究探討，特別是隨着近百年來考古學的發展，青銅器學中已解決了多數器類的定名及用途問題。一些器類因爲本身有自銘，而且見於文獻的記載，加之又有考古資料的佐證，其定名與用途已無異議。如鼎類器，不僅常見其自銘爲"鼎"，器形也與《説文》中"鼎，三足，兩耳"的描述一致；考古發現中不少鼎的器底、三足都帶有明顯的煙炱痕迹，這就證明了《玉篇》所謂鼎是"所以熟食器也"的表述；而考古資料中一些鼎出土時器腹內尚存有牛、羊、猪骨，這與《周禮·天官·亨人》鄭玄注中所謂"鑊，所以煮肉及魚臘之器，既熟乃脀於鼎"的解釋是一致的，表明鼎同時兼具盛食器的功用，這樣就從諸多方面確定了鼎的定名及用途。

圖四 （拓片／李孔融）

圖五

但是仍有部分器類的定名與用途迄今尚未解決，如我們現在稱之爲觚的這類器物。這種大敞口長斜頸直筒腹斜坡形高圈足的銅器，從未發現有自銘器名，稱其爲觚是由宋人《考古圖》中所定，沿用至今。器名的不確定，使得對其用途的研究也就缺少了由文獻入手的途徑，現在一般只是根據器形及相關考古資料做推論。觚的形制有如酒杯，在商周時期的考古資料中，其與爵通常都是成對出土的，它們構成了當時，特別是商代晚期青銅禮器組合中的基本內容。這一現象表明觚與爵在使用上必定存在一定的關聯，容庚、張維持先生認爲："如需温酒而飲則用爵，不需温酒而飲則用觚"[16]，這就肯定了觚是飲酒器。

朱鳳瀚先生在《古代中國青銅器》一書中雖將觚歸於飲酒器類，但他引用林巳奈夫先生在《殷周時代青銅器之研究·殷周青銅器綜覽一》中的研究意見："在殷中期時，觚口部張開程度不大，用作酒杯是可以的……。但到殷後期時，觚大口極度外張，且器腹小而容量少，此種形制如仍用來飲酒，則酒很容易灑出來，所以不適合再盛液體了。他估計此種大口極度外張的觚乃專用以盛甜酒（醴），

16.容庚、張維持《殷周青銅器通論》第62頁，文物出版社1984年版。

圖六

用柶（匙）舀取而食，引《儀禮·士冠禮》言'冠者即筵坐。左執觶，右祭脯醢，以柶祭醴三，興，筵末坐。啐醴，建柶興……'爲證"。並指出林巳奈夫還以商代晚期銅尊銘文中的象形圖案爲證（圖五），認爲其中"人形手持觚，其上即有一垂直匙形器放於腹中，認爲此當即如上引《士冠禮》所言於盛醴的酒器中建柶之形。……器銘圖像中似觚（或觚形尊）中所插立者確是柶一類挹取器，則上述林巳奈夫對殷代大口極張的觚用以盛醴之推測有相當道理。"[17]《周禮·天官·酒正》："二曰醴齊"鄭玄注："醴，猶體也，成而汁滓相將，如今恬酒矣。"可見醴猶如今日之酒釀，故林巳奈夫先生認爲需用匙舀取而食。但商代晚期的觚形器雖口部極其侈張，其容器部分却漸收成細筒形，如盛放接近固態類的酒釀，再用匙形器舀取而食，恐怕並不便利，此說值得商榷。

春秋晚期和戰國時期，在青銅器上出現的畫像紋中常有表現宴樂場面的內容，其中就常見有人用柶從壺形器往觚挹酒，並執觚敬賓客的場景，如上海博物館藏宴樂畫像紋杯[18]、保利博物館藏畫像紋壺[19]、成都百花潭出土畫像紋壺[20]等。

首陽齋藏戰國宴射畫像刻紋匜，內壁鏨刻有畫像紋，內容也以當時流行的射禮、宴樂爲主，雖然與其他一些青銅器上的畫像紋相比，該匜的畫像紋稍顯簡略，但就我們討論觚形器的作用而言，它就非常重要。在這件匜流部下的內壁上鏨刻了一組圖案（圖六），從左至右分別是一人執觚躬身敬客，對立一人則欠身以對；中間一案上放置兩個壺形器，一人執觚欲往盛酒，另一人則執柶從壺中往觚裏舀酒；最右面是兩人相對跽坐於地，其中一人正執觚作飲酒狀。這組畫像說明兩個問題，第一，在當時柶是用作挹酒于觚的，而不是用來從觚中舀取而食的；第二，觚是可以用作飲酒的。

可以認爲，首陽齋所藏這件宴射畫像刻紋匜的內容，是迄今爲止能够證明觚形器爲飲酒器最直接最可靠的依據。就此而言，這件匜就彌足珍貴了。

2008年5月28日完稿於上海博物館

17.朱鳳瀚《古代中國青銅器》第119頁，南開大學出版社1995年版。

18.馬承源《漫談戰國青銅器上的畫像》，《文物》1961年第10期第26頁。

19.保利藝術博物館《保利藏金》（續）第186頁，嶺南美術出版社2001年版。

20.四川省博物館《成都百花潭中學十號墓發掘記》，《文物》1976年第3期第40頁，圖版二。

Notes on Bronzes from the Shouyang Studio Collection

Zhou Ya

According to Mr. George Fan, he grew up and was educated in the West. After he was introduced to the world of ancient Chinese bronzes, Mr. Fan was deeply attracted to the rich cultural and historical context of these objects. In order to enrich their understanding in Chinese history and culture, Mr. and Mrs. Fan began to collect Chinese bronzes. Apart from specializing on bronzes with inscriptions, Mr. Fan aims at assembling a more comprehensive collection spanning the Xia, Shang and Zhou periods. His bronze collection, though not huge in terms of quantity, features representative examples of all the major periods, together they illuminate the development of ancient Chinese bronzes. For the present exhibition at the Shanghai Museum, Mr. and Mrs. George Fan specially select 70 items of bronzes from their collection. With great pleasure, we have examined all these objects in close quarters. This essay is a very preliminary account of what we can observe from these bronzes.

I

Early Chinese bronzes have drawn much attention of scholars due to their connections with the origin of Chinese bronze casting technique and the forming of a ritual bronze system. Such early bronze wares as knives, awls, chisels, axes, mirrors and ornaments have been found from the sites of the Majiayao Culture and the Qijia Culture in Gansu and Qinghai Provinces, but all of them were cast in a single mould or forged. It is generally accepted that bronze vessels cast in composite or sectional moulds marked the beginning of Chinese bronze technology *per se*. The earliest intact bronze vessels we have seen so far were mainly unearthed from the sites of the Erlitou Culture which is dated to the late Xia period when Chinese bronze casting was created. Therefore, every piece of bronze from this period is very important to the research of the origin of Chinese bronze casting.

According to *Zhongguo Kaoguxue:Xia Shang juan* published in 2003, totally eighteen bronze vessels were excavated from the Erlitou Culture site in Yanshi, Henan Province, which include thirteen *jue*, three *jia*, a *ding* as well as a *he*. A small number of bronze vessels, such as *jue* and *jia*, were unearthed from other sites of the Erlitou Culture. In addition, a few bronze vessels dated to the same period are extant in some museums (Zhongguo 2003: p.109).

In the Shouyang Studio collection is a *jue* cast in the characteristic form and style of the Erlitou Culture. This vessel has a narrow spout, a short and wide tail, a waisted belly, a flat base and three conical legs. A flange can be seen on the rim inside. The semicircular handle with openwork links the rim and the base. There is a raised triangle at the joint of the legs and the belly, which is also seen on a jue with a tube-shaped spout, also known as jiao, of the Erlitou Culture period found in Luoning, Henan Province in 1980 (Zhongguo Qingtongqi 1996: p.11). On one side of the belly are two raised lines which have never been seen on any other jue of the Erlitou period before (fig.1). Whether this is meant for decorative purpose, for strengthening the belly, or for both purposes, is worthy of note.

The *jue* of Erlitou can generally be classified into two types. One is primitive in style, with strong influence from the contemporary earthenware *jue*; the other, in refined form and detail, reveals the originality of bronze *jue*. According to Professor Du Jinpeng, the first type dated from the third phase of the Erlitou Culture, and the second type from the fourth phase (Du Jinpeng 1994: p.263). They attest to a period of rapid technological development. The Erlitou *jue* of the Shouyang Studio closely resembles a *jue* unearthed from an Erlitou site (VIII T22③:6) in 1973, hence, it belongs, archaeologically, to the third phase of the Erlitou Culture.

Bronze vessels dated to the lower stratum (early period) of the Erligang Culture, which followed the Erlitou Culture, have drawn much attention of scholars due to their significance in the development of bronze casting technology and in the transformation of the ritual bronze system from the Xia dynasty to the Shang period. However, only a few examples of this period have been unearthed. According to *Zhengzhou Shangcheng*, the eleven bronze vessels of three different types including *jia*, *jue* and *he* dated to the second phase of the lower stratum provide the earliest examples of Erligang bronzes from Shangcheng, Zhengzhou to date (Henan 2001: p.674).

An early Shang *jia* with linked circles in the Shouyang Studio collection closely resembles the one published in *Chinese Bronzes:A Selection from European Collections*, which is dated to the Erlitou Culture. Yet the authors remark that the legs of the *jia* are short and the belly is similar to that of the early Shang *jia*, suggesting that it might belong to a later period (Li Xueqin and Sarah Allan 1995: p.311, black-and-white pl.2). In our opinion, this *jia* of the Shouyang Studio is of a similar shape to a bronze *jia* unearthed from the second phase of the lower stratum of the Erligang Culture at Baijiazhuang, Zhengzhou, Henan Province. Furthermore, the hollow linked circles on the neck are often seen on Erligang bronzes, while Erlitou bronzes are usually decorated with solid linked bosses. Thus, we think the *jia* was cast in the early Shang period. On the other hand, the pillars on its rim are in the form of a trihedral nail, often seen on the *jia* vessels of the Erlitou Culture, for instance, the *jia* unearthed in 1984 (Zhongguo 1986: p.318) from a burial (M9) at the Erlitou site in Yanshi, Henan and another one excavated subsequently in 1987 (87TLVM1) (Zhongguo 1991: p.1138). This type of pillar is different from that of Erligang bronzes which basically takes the form of a square mushroom. Therefore, we consider this *jia* an example illustrating the period of transition from the Erlitou Culture to the Erligang Culture. It is a rare specimen and is particularly important to the research on the transformation of bronze *jia* from Erlitou to Erligang.

II

Two items of cylindrical vessels or beakers in the collection of the Shouyang Studio are very interesting. One is a five-piece set with no decoration. They are in the same shape but in progressively reduced sizes, and the biggest one has a cover. The other item, in the same shape as the nesting set, is decorated with intertwined dragons in three sections.

Only a few bronzes of this type have been found in archaeological excavations, including a five-piece set unearthed from Sanji, Pingshan County, Hebei Province (Liu Yunhua 1996: p.83), two pieces from a burial at Zangjiazhuang, Zhucheng County, Shandong Province (Shandong 1987: p.47), one piece without a lid from a burial at Yuehe, Tongbai County, Henan Province (Nanyang 1997: p.8), one piece from the burial of Liu Sheng, the Prince of Zhongshan Principality in Mancheng County, Hebei Province (Zhongguo 1980:vol.1, p.78), one piece from a Han burial at Luobowan, Gui County, Guangxi Province (Guangxi 1988: p.36), and one more in the Shanghai Museum collection. Additionally, Minao Hayashi records two cylindrical vessels in his book *Shujunsenkoku jiki seidoki no kenkyuu* (Studies on the Bronzes of the Spring and Autumn and Warring States Periods), but does not mention the provenance. Most of these bronzes have no decoration except the ones from the Shanghai Museum and the burial of Liu Sheng, the former with cowry and plaited designs and the latter with lozenged birds. Some of them have ring handles. In particular, one of Minao Hayashi's examples has an animal handle on the lower part of the belly, resembling the *lei* wine container of the Shang period.

The above mentioned beakers are called differently as '*bei*'(cup), '*bei xing hu*'(cup-shaped vase), '*tong bei*'(cylindrical cup), '*he*'(box) or '*chang hu*'(tall vase). This is because scholars have different opinions on the use of the vessel. *Bei* is a wine drinking vessel, while *hu* is a wine container. As far as we are concerned with the function of such a vessel, it is important to study closely the form. A table of these cylindrical vessels is attached at the end of the essay.

The beakers can be divided into two types: one has ring handles and the other not. The former is usually 32.4 to 43.4cm high, and the latter 14.5 to 22.7cm high. If the latter could be used for drinking wine, the height of the former would not meet this need. In addition, most of the bronze vessels with lids were used as containers, not for drinking wine.

It is noteworthy that besides the gilt bronze beakers with lozenged birds a set of five nesting gilt bronze cups with the same motifs were also recovered from the burial of Prince Liu Sheng in Mancheng. According to the archaeological report, these cups and the beakers were put together inside the tomb, showing that they were meant to be used together. Now that cups were used for drinking wine, beakers should be wine containers. In addition, the capacity of the beakers found in Mancheng is about 200ml, which is very close to that of one of the five cups (196ml). Thus, we strongly believe that five beakers with matching cups were cast but only one was buried in Liu Sheng's burial due to some unknown reasons.

Since the beaker was not a wine cup but a container, it should not be called '*bei*'. It is not proper to call it '*chang hu*' or '*bei xing hu*' as *hu* (vase) of the Shang and Zhou periods basically has a small mouth, a neck, a bulging belly and a foot-ring, which is well-illustrated by the pictogram of *hu* in bronze inscriptions (fig. 2). The cylindrical vessel, having a wide mouth and a straight profile tapering towards a foot-ring, is markedly different. Therefore, we prefer calling it '*tong xing qi*' (cylindrical vessel) before further evidence for naming such a vessel is available.

The decoration of intertwined dragons on a cylindrical vessel in the Shouyang Studio collection is often seen on the bronze *ding* of the mid to late Warring States period, such as a *ding* excavated from Miaozhuang, Pingliang, Gansu Province (Wei Huaiheng 1982: p.27), the Zhong Min *ding* and the Ping *ding* from Ta'erpo, Xianyang, Shaanxi Province (Xianyang 1975: p.69) as well as two types of *ding* from a Eastern Zhou burial in Luoyang, Henan Province (Luoyang 2001: p.41). The forms of these *ding* indicate that they were all cast in the capital area of Eastern Zhou or within the States of Han, Zhao and Wei.

The beaker of the Shanghai Museum (fig.3) has a lid with four phoenix-shaped knobs and designs of rope and shell. The body is also decorated with alternating ropes and shell bands. These two decorative motifs are very common on bronzes of the Han, Zhao and Wei States of the Warring States period. Some clay moulds with rope and shell designs have been discovered from a bronze foundry in Houma, Shanxi Province (fig.4).

While the vessel from Tongbai, Henan Province is dated from the Spring and Autumn period, those found in Mancheng, Hebei Province and Guixian, Guangxi Province belong to the early Western Han. The rest of the above-mentioned beakers are bronzes of the mid to late Warring States period. These bronzes were made mostly in the Central Plains but there are exceptions, as there are two examples from Southwest China in the area of Chu culture.

III

Through studies by many scholars over the years and with the development of archaeology in China in the recent century, the naming and uses of most bronzes have been solved. In some cases typological names are recorded in the inscriptions (known as 'self-naming') on the bronzes, and are verified by historical texts and archaeological evidences, for example, *ding*. Firstly, the Chinese character '*ding*' have been inscribed on many *ding* vessels as a self-naming evidence. Secondly, same as the description in *Shuowen Jiezi* by Xu Shen of the Eastern Han dynasty, the *ding* vessel has three legs and two handles. Thirdly, black traces of heating over fire observable at the bases and legs of some *ding* vessels are evident that the *ding* was a cooking utensil. Fourthly, some *ding* cauldrons still contained the bones of oxen, goats and pigs when they were unearthed, showing that they were also food containers.

The names and uses of some bronzes, such as the *gu*, have not been confirmed. Known generally as a vessel with a wide mouth, a flaring long neck, a cylindrical body and a splayed high foot-ring, however, not even one *gu* has been found inscribed with a typological name. The term '*gu*' originated from *Kaogu Tu* (Illustrations to Antiques) of the Song dynasty and has been used thereafter. Speaking of its use, scholars can only draw inferences from its form and related archaeological materials, not from writing of earlier periods due to the lack of a verified typological name. Shaped like a wine cup, *gu* was usually excavated together with *jue*, which indicates that there is a correlation between the two in terms of their uses. Rong Geng and Zhang Weichi noted in their book that these were wine cups serving different purposes, namely the wine in a *jue* would be heated up (Rong Geng and Zhang Weichi 1984: p.62).

In his book *Gudai Zhongguo qingtongqi* (Ancient Chinese Bronzes) published in 1995, Zhu Fenghan cited the opinion of Minao Hayashi that during the mid Shang dynasty, *gu* with a slight flared mouth could be used as a wine cup; but the wide flaring mouth and the small body of the late Shang *gu* could no longer serve the purpose of drinking (Zhu Fenghan 1995: p.119). Minao Hayashi thought that this kind of *gu* with such a wide mouth would be used to contain a thick and sweet alcoholic drink with the fermented glutinous rice called *li* in ancient China, which had to be taken with *si*, a spoon. He used a pictographic from the inscription of a late Shang bronze *zun* vase as evidence (fig.5). However, it seems really hard to spoon the contents from the small cylindrical body of the late Shang *gu*. Minao Hayashi's opinion needs further verification.

Bronzes of the late Spring and Autumn and the Warring States periods are frequently decorated with banquet scenes, which have in common people filling a *gu* with wine taken from a *hu* vase by using a *si* and people presenting the *gu* to guests, to name but a few, a cup in the Shanghai Museum collection (Ma Chengyuan 1961: p.26), a *hu* in the Poly Art Museum collection (Baoli 2001: p.186) and another *hu* unearthed from Baihuatan, Chengdu, Sichuan Province (Sichuan 1976: p.47, pl.2).

In the Shouyang Studio collection is a *yi* water vessel with banquet and hunting scenes of the Warring States period. Although the depiction of this *yi* looks simpler than that of other bronzes featuring similar decorative scenes, it is exceptionally important regarding the use of *gu*. A group of three narrative scenes are engraved below the spout in the interior of the *yi* (fig.6). On the left is a man bowing and offering a *gu* to a guest. In the middle is a table with two *hu* vases on it, where a man uses a *si* to spoon wine from the *hu*. Another man is walking to the table to fill the *gu* in his hand. On the right are two men sitting on their heels, and one of them is drinking wine with a *gu*. These scenes reveal two facts: first, *si* was used for filling the *gu* with wine, but not the other way round; second, *gu* could be used for drinking wine.

To conclude, the *yi* of the Shouyang Studio is particularly important as it provides the most tangible and convincing evidence that *gu* is a wine-drinking vessel to date.

No.	Object	Provenance	Height (cm)	Mouth Diameter (cm)	Description	Remarks
1	Cylindrical vessel	Shouyang Studio	14.8	5.6	Lid with three ring knobs; no ring handles	A five-piece set
2	Cylindrical vessel	Shouyang Studio	22.7	9	Lid with three ring knobs; no ring handles	
3	Cylindrical vessel	Pingshan, Hebei	15	5.8	Lid with three ring knobs; no ring handles	A five-piece set
4	Cylindrical vessel	Mancheng, Hebei	14.5	5.5	Ring knob; no ring handles	
5	Cylindrical vessel	Tongbai, Henan	17.7	9.3	No ring handles	Lid lost
6	Cylindrical vessel	Zhucheng, Shandong	32.9	11.5	Lid with three ring knobs; ring handles	
7	Cylindrical vessel	Guixian, Guangxi	39.3	13.6	Lid with four ring knobs; ring handles	
8	Cylindrical vessel	Shanghai Museum	32	11.3	Ring handles with animal marks; lid with four bird knobs	
9	Cylindrical vessel	Minao Hayashi	32.4		Lid with four ring knobs ring handles	
10	Cylindrical vessel	Minao Hayashi	43.4		Ring handles with animal marks; lid with four animal-shaped knobs; animal-shaped handle	

References

Baoli 2001
Baoli Yishu Bowuguan, *Baoli cangjin* (Bronzes from the Poly Art Museum), Guangzhou:Lingnan Meishu chubanshe, 2001.

Du Jinpeng 1994
Du Jinpeng, 'Shang Zhou tong jue yanjiu', *Kaogu xuebao*, 1994.3.

Guangxi 1988
Guangxi Zhuangzu Zizhiqu Bowuguan, *Guangxi Gaixian Luobowan Han mu* (Luobowan Han Tombs in Guixian County), Beijing:Wenwu chubanshe, 1988.

Henan 2001
Henan Sheng Wenwu Kaogu Yanjiusuo, *Zhengzhou Shangcheng* (The Site of Shang Dynasty City in Zhengzhou), 3 vols, Beijing:Wenwu chubanshe, 2001.

Liu Yunhua 1996
Liu Yunhua, 'Qingtong taobei he taobo', *Wenwu chunqiu*, 1996.1.

Li Xueqin and Sarah Allan 1995
Xueqin Li and Sarah Allan, *Ouzhou suocang Zhongguo qingtongqi yizhu* (Chinese Bronzes: A Selection from European Collections), Beijing:Wenwu chubanshe, 1995.

Luoyang 2001
Luoyang Shi Wenwu Gongzuodui, 'Luoyang shi zhenzhichang Dongzhou mu (C1M5269) de qingli', *Wenwu*, 2001.12.

Ma Chengyuan 1961
Ma Chengyuan, 'Mantan Zhanguo qingtongqi shang de huaxiang', *Wenwu*, 1961.10.

Nanyang 1997
Nanyang Shi Wenwu Yanjiusuo and Tongbai Xian Wenguanban, 'Tongbai Yuehe yihao mu fajue jianbao', *Zhongyuan wenwu*, 1997.4.

Rong Geng and Zhang Weichi 1984
Rong Geng and Zhang Weichi, *Yin Zhou qingtongqi ton glun* (General Introduction to Shang and Zhou Bronzes), Beijing:Wenwu chubanshe, 1984.

Shandong 1987
Shandong Zhucheng Xian Bowuguan, 'Shandong Zhucheng Zangjiazhuang yu Gebukoucun Zhanguo mu', *Wenwu*, 1987.12.

Sichuan 1976
Sichuan Sheng Bownguan, 'Chengdu Baihuatan zhongxue shihao mu fajue ji', *Wenwu*, 1976.3.

Wei Huaiheng 1982
Wei Huaiheng, 'Gansu Pingliang Miaozhuang de liang zuo Zhanguo mu', *Kaogu yu wenwu*, 1982.5.

Xianyang 1975
Xianyang Shi Bowuguan, 'Shaanxi Xianyang Ta'erpo chutu de tongqi', *Wenwu*, 1975.6.

Zhongguo 1980
Zhongguo Shehui Kexueyuan Kaogu Yanjiusuo and Hebei Sheng Wenwu Guanlichu, *Mancheng Han mu fajue jianbao* (Excavation of the Han Tombs at Man-cheng), 2 vols, Beijing:Wenwu chubanshe, 1980.

Zhongguo 1986
Zhongguo Shehui Kexueyuan Kaogu Yanjiusuo Erlitou Gongzuodui, '1984 nian qiu Henan Yanshi Erlitou yizhi faxian de jizuo muzang', *Kaogu*, 1986.4.

Zhongguo 1991
Zhongguo Shehui Kexueyuan Kaogu Yanjiusuo Erlitou Gongzuodui, 'Henan Yanshi Erlitou yizhi faxian xin de tongqi', *Kaogu*, 1991.12.

Zhongguo 2003
Zhongguo Shehui Kexueyuan Kaogu Yanjiusuo, *Zhongguo Kaoguxue, Xia Shang juan* (Chinese Archaeology:Xia and Shang), Beijing:Zhongguo shehui kexue chubanshe, 2003.

Zhongguo Qingtongqi 1996
Zhongguo Qingtongqi Quanji Bianji Weiyuanhui, *Zhongguo qingtonqi quanji* (A Comprehensive Collection of Chinese Bronzes), vol.1, Beijing:Wenwu chubanshe, 1996.

Zhu Fenghan 1995
Zhu Fenghan. *Gudai Zhongguo qingtongqi* (Ancient Chinese Bronzes), Tianjin:Nankai daxue chubanshe, 1995.

圖版及展品説明
Plates and Catalogue Entries

1

爵

夏代晚期（公元前18世紀－前16世紀）

高14.6厘米　流至尾長7.2厘米　腹深8.3厘米　腹徑4.2厘米　重262.8克

　　爵是中國最早出現的青銅禮器之一，在河南偃師二里頭遺址及周邊新鄭、商丘一帶的二里頭文化遺址中都曾有陸續出土。有學者指出：“二里頭遺址所發現的銅器墓中，如果只出一件青銅容器便必定爲爵，若有兩件或更多的銅容器，其中必有爵”[1]。由此可見，爵是當時禮制中最基本和最主要的器物，在青銅體制初創之時便具有非常重要的作用。故早在宋代的《博古圖》中就指出：爵雖小，然“在禮實大”。

　　這件爵作窄流、寬短尾、束腰、平底、三錐足的樣式，口緣內側有一周凸邊，半環形鋬自口沿直至腹底，鋬上有鏤孔。足與腹底連接處有三角錐形凸出，這種現象與1980年河南洛寧出土的一件二里頭時期管流爵（或稱之爲角）相似[2]。

　　爵的形制與1973年二里頭遺址三期文化中出土的一件青銅爵（ⅧT22③:6）[3]非常接近，應該也是屬於這一時期的青銅製品。

　　在爵腹一側，有兩條隨器腹束放走向而設的凸起弧綫，這是我們在以往二里頭時期青銅爵上沒有注意到的現象。

Jue (wine vessel)

Late Xia (18th – 16th century BC)

Height 14.6cm, overall length 7.2cm, depth 8.3cm, diameter of belly 4.2cm, weight 262.8g

As one of the earliest ritual bronze vessels in China, *jue* has been discovered at Erlitou in Yanshi, Henan Province, and also unearthed from other sites of the Erlitou culture in Xinzheng and Shangqiu. Scholars pointed out that at Erlitou sites, if there was only one piece of bronze vessel found in a burial, it must be a *jue*; if two or more bronze vessels were found, *jue* must be included (Du Jinpeng 1994:p.287). This means *jue* had been a most essential vessel in the ancient ritual bronze system since inception. The *Bogu Tu* (Illustrated Catalogue of Antiquities) of the Song dynasty also mentioned that *jue*, although small in form, played an important role in the ritual system.

This *jue* has a narrow spout, a short tail, a contracted belly with flat bottom, three conical legs and a bifurcated handle. Along the inner rim there is a raised edge. At the joint of the legs and the bottom are protruding ridges which are similar to a *jue* with a tube-shaped spout (also known as *jiao*) unearthed from Luoning, Henan Province in 1980 (Zhongguo Qingtongqi 1996:pl.11).

This *jue* is similar in shape to a *jue* (VIII22③:6) excavated in 1973 and dated to the third phase of Erlitou culture (Zhongguo 1975:p.302). The two pieces should belong to the same period. However, two raised bands were cast on the one side of the belly of this *jue*-a feature not seen on *Erlitou* bronzes.

---

1. 杜金鵬《商周銅爵研究》，《考古學報》1994年第3期第287頁。

2. 中國青銅器全集編輯委員會《中國青銅器全集·1》圖版一一，文物出版社1996年版。

3. 中國科學院考古研究所二里頭工作隊《河南偃師二里頭遺址三、八區發掘簡報》，《考古》1975年第5期第302頁。

23

聯珠紋斝　商代早期（公元前16世紀－前15世紀中葉）
高21.1厘米　口徑14.8厘米　腹深11.2厘米　腹徑10.9厘米　重742.3克

　　在二里頭文化遺址中就出土有青銅斝，表明斝也是中國最早出現的青銅禮器之一。這件斝敞口，口沿立有兩個三棱形釘形柱；高頸，斜折腹，腹側有環形鋬；平底下承四棱形錐足，足部中空。兩柱間頸部一側飾有空心聯珠紋一道，上下有兩道弦紋爲欄。

　　《歐洲所藏中國青銅器遺珠》著錄有一件與此非常相似的聯珠紋斝，作者認爲屬於二里頭文化時期，但同時也指出"此器錐足較短，腹形更接近商代前期的斝，年代也可能稍晚一些"[1]。我們認爲這件斝的三棱形釘形柱確實與二里頭文化遺址出土的青銅斝之柱相同，但整體形制上更接近於河南鄭州白家莊商代二里岡下層二期出土的青銅斝[2]。且三足近乎直立的設計，與早期青銅三足器一般足部外撇有異，而與二里岡下層文化遺址中出土青銅爵的足部作直立狀的形式相近似。此外，斝頸部一側裝飾的空心聯珠紋，也是商代二里岡時期才開始在青銅器上運用得比較多的一種紋樣，二里頭文化時期青銅器上裝飾的一般都是實心聯珠紋。由此，我們認爲這件斝應該還是屬於二里岡下層文化時期的青銅器，亦即商代早期的青銅器。

***Jia* (wine vessel) with linked circles**

Early Shang (16th – mid 15th century BC)
Height 21.1cm, diameter of mouth 14.8cm, depth 11.2cm, diameter of belly 10.9cm, weight 742.3g

Jia occurs among the bronzes unearthed from the Erlitou site, indicating that it was also one of the earliest ritual vessels. This *jia* has two nail-shaped pillars of triangular section set on the flaring mouth rim, a long neck, and a handle attached to the angular belly, supported by three hollow, conical legs. On one side of the neck is decorated with a band of hollow, linked circles between two bow strings.

A very similar *jia* in a European collection has been published in *Ouzhou suocang Zhongguo qingtonqi yizhu* (Li Xueqin and Sarah Allan 1995:p.311, black and white pl.2). While it is dated to the Erlitou Culture as well, the authors noted that its legs are shorter and its belly is similar to that of early Shang. In our opinion, the nail-shaped pillars on this vessel are indeed in the Erlitou style, but the *jia*'s shape, especially the vertical leg, is close to the bronze *jia* unearthed from the lower stratum of the Erligang Culture at Baijiazhuang, Zhengzhou, Henan Province (Henan 2001:p.674, colour pl.9.1). Moreover, the hollow, linked circles appear on bronzes in the Erligang period as well, while a solid linked- bosses are found on bronzes from Erlitou. So we suggest this *jia* should belong to the lower stratum (early period) of the Erligang Culture, that is, early Shang dynasty.

1.李學勤、艾蘭《歐洲所藏中國青銅器遺珠》黑白圖版二、第311頁，文物出版社1995年版。
2.河南省文物考古研究所《鄭州商城》（中）第674頁；（下）彩版九·1，文物出版社2001年版。

3

弦紋爵

商代早期（公元前16世紀－前15世紀中葉）

高14.7厘米　流至尾11.6厘米　腹深6.4厘米　腹徑6.7厘米　重250.7克

　　流部微曲上昂，尖短尾，口沿有加厚的唇邊。直腰，鼓腹，平底，直立的棱形錐足較細長。腰部飾三道凸起的弦紋。流口連接處設兩個釘狀柱，柱頂部作月牙形，商代早期青銅爵之釘狀柱上常見這樣月牙形的設計，如鄭州白家莊二里岡下層二期出土的青銅爵（C8采:豫文104）[1]，白家莊二里岡上層一期墓葬出土的弦紋爵（C11M125:1）和鄭州北二七路墓葬出土的三角紋爵（BQM2:2）[2]，以及湖北黃陂盤龍城李家嘴2號墓出土的兩件爵（PLZM2:11，PLZM2:23）[3]等。

　　這件爵比較接近於鄭州二里岡上層一期出土的弦紋爵（C11M125:1）和盤龍城李家嘴2號墓出土的弦紋爵（PLZM2:23），應該是同一時期的器物。

Jue (wine vessel) with bow-string pattern

Early Shang (16th – mid 15th century BC)

Height 14.7cm, overall length 11.6cm, depth 6.4cm, diameter of belly 6.7cm, weight 250.7g

This *jue* has a slanting spout, a short and pointed tail, a thickened mouth rim and a bulging belly with a flat bottom resting on three vertical and conical legs. Three raised bow-strings were decorated around the neck. At the joint of the spout and mouth are two nail-shaped pillars with crescent-formed caps. This design of pillar was always used on early Shang bronze *jue* vessels, such as one (C8 *Cai:Yuwen*104) from the second phase of the lower Erligang Culture, unearthed from Baijiazhuang in Zhengzhou (Henan 2001:p.674,fig.462.4),

a *jue* with bow-string pattern (C11M125:1) of the first phase of the upper Erligang Culture found at Baijiazhuang, a *jue* with triangle pattern (BQM2:2) excavated from a burial on Bei'erqi Road, Zhengzhou (Henan 2001:p.809, fig.545.5; p.811, fig.546.9) as well as a *jue* (PLZM2:11, PLZM2:23) from No.2 burial at Lijiazui in Panlongcheng, Huangpi, Hubei Province (Hubei 2001:vol. 1, p.163, figs.105.1 and 105.5). Thus, the current vessel should be of the same period as those mentioned above.

1.河南省文物考古研究所《鄭州商城》（中）第674頁，圖四六二‧4，文物出版社2001年版。

2.同上第809頁，圖五四五‧5；第811頁，圖五四六‧9。

3.湖北省文物考古研究所《盤龍城——1963～1994年考古發掘報告》（上）第163頁，圖一〇五‧1，圖一〇五‧5，文物出版社2001年版。

4

弦紋扁足鼎

商代早期（公元前16世紀–前15世紀中葉）

高18.3厘米　口徑12.9厘米　腹深9.1厘米　腹徑11.8厘米　重658.2克

　　扁足鼎是青銅鼎形器中之一類，主要出現在商代和西周早期。扁足鼎以圓鼎爲主，偶見方鼎，扁足圓鼎有深腹圓底和淺腹圓底兩種，前者僅見於商代早、中期，後者雖貫穿於扁足鼎之始終，但以商代晚期和西周早期最爲多見。扁足的形式以扁平刀形和近乎圓雕動物形爲主，通常用龍、鳳形象作爲扁足的式樣。考古發現中，扁足鼎的出土並不多見，一般是單個出土的。安陽殷墟5號墓中出土扁足鼎共五件，一件是扁足方鼎，四件扁足圓鼎，但其中有三件屬同一組扁足鼎[1]。江西新干大洋洲商墓出土有扁足鼎十四件，大致可分爲四種不同的式樣[2]。這是出土扁足鼎數量最多，資料最爲豐富的兩個墓葬。

　　這件扁足鼎作深腹圓底的式樣，兩耳與三足作四點式分佈，即一足與一耳位於同一垂直綫上，這是早期青銅鼎、鬲上耳、足位置的普遍現象。扁平刀形的三足作直立變形龍紋，龍口張開承托鼎腹，這是扁足鼎足部通常所用的裝飾樣式。鼎的一耳及腹底有當時補鑄的痕迹，這是早期青銅器上常見現象，表明當時的青銅鑄造技術尚處在成長發展時期。

　　考古發掘及傳世的扁足鼎，一般都裝飾有獸面紋等紋樣，這件鼎的腹部只裝飾兩條弦紋。雖然只裝飾弦紋在早期青銅器中是常見的現象，但在當時的扁足鼎中並不多見，僅湖北黃陂盤龍城李家嘴2號墓出土一件裝飾弦紋的扁足鼎[3]。

Ding (food vessel) with bow-string pattern and flat legs

Early Shang (16th – mid 15th century BC)

Height 18.3cm, diameter of mouth 12.9cm, depth 9.1cm, diameter of belly 11.8cm, weight 658.2g

This *ding* form, with flat legs, appeared in the Shang and early Western Zhou periods. The globular bowl, or more rarely, rectangular bowl may be deep or shallow. The round *ding* form with a deep belly was only cast in early and mid Shang, while the shallow one was popular during late Shang to early Western Zhou. The flat legs are mainly cast in the shape of blades or animals like dragons and phoenixes.

Not many *ding* with flat legs have been found from archaeological excavations. Normally, only one piece was unearthed from a burial, but there were also exceptions. Five *ding* with flat legs were found from No.5 burial at the Yin Ruins in Anyang, Henan Province, including a rectangular *ding* and four round ones (Zhongguo 1980a:p.44). Another fourteen pieces in four types have been excavated from a Shang burial at Dayangzhou in Xingan, Jiangxi Province.

This deep *ding* has a globular body with two handles and three leaf-blade legs cast in the form of stylized dragons. One of the handles and a leg are arranged vertically in a line, which is a common phenomenon on early bronze *ding* and *li*. Additionally, remedial castings are found at the *ding*'s bottom and one of the handles, indicating that the casting technique was not perfected at that time.

1.中國社會科學院考古研究所《殷墟婦好墓》第44頁，文物出版社1980年版。

2.江西省文物考古研究所等《新干商代大墓》第18頁，圖版五、六、七、八，文物出版社1997年版。

3.湖北省文物考古研究所《盤龍城——1963～1994年考古發掘報告》（上）第171頁，圖一一三‧3，文物出版社2001年版。

Most *ding* with flat legs are usually decorated with animal masks, but this one only bears two bow strings on the belly. It is similar to another *ding* unearthed from No.2 burial at Lijiazui in Panlongcheng, Huangpi, Hubei Province (Hubei 2001:vol.1, p.171, fig.113.3).

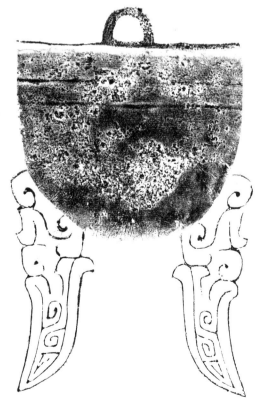

5

弦紋鬲

商代早期（公元前16世紀－前15世紀中葉）
高17.8厘米　口徑14.5厘米　腹深11.8厘米　腹徑14.2厘米　重1181.1克

　　鬲是中國古代最常使用的炊器之一，在新石器時期陶鬲就被普遍使用。商代早期出現青銅鬲，之後它幾乎行用於整個青銅時代。根據記載，鬲一般用於炊煮粥類食物，但從考古資料來看，鬲也可用於盛放肉類食物。早期青銅鬲的造型與鼎相似，都是深圓腹，兩耳，三足。但是它的腹底與鼎不同，它的腹下部做成由三個圓袋形相合的式樣，故腹底形成三叉形凹槽，在每一個袋形腹的下面連接一個錐足。這樣的設計是爲了擴大受火的面積，加快食物的炊煮過程。

　　這件鬲平折口沿上有一周加厚的唇邊，略鼓出的深袋腹下接三個四棱形空心錐足，兩耳與三足也作四點式分佈，頸部有弦紋一道。鬲的形制與鄭州楊莊二里岡上層一期墓葬中出土X紋鬲（C2：豫0013）非常接近[1]。鬲的表面銹蝕嚴重，隱約能看到數道微凸的斜弦紋，有可能原本飾有類似的X紋或人字形紋。

Li (food vessel) with bow-string pattern

Early Shang (16th – mid 15th century BC)
Height 17.8cm, diameter of mouth 14.5cm, depth 11.8cm, diameter of belly 14.2cm, weight 1181.1g

Li is one kind of popular cooking vessels used in ancient China. In the Neolithic age, earthenware li was common. Bronze li appeared in the early Shang, and continued through the whole Bronze Age. According to historical records, li was used for cooking congee, but archeological evidences have proved that it could be also used as a meat container. In the early periods the shape of bronze li was similar to that of ding, which has a deep globular body with two handles and three legs. However, differing from ding, the bottom of li was cast in the shape of three pouches supported on three conical legs to increase the heating surfaces and to speed up the cooking process.

This li has an everted and thickened rim, a deep pouch-shaped belly and three hollow, conical legs. Its neck is decorated with bow-string pattern. The vessel can compare to a li with X pattern excavated from a burial in Erligang of Yangzhuang, Zhengzhou, Henan Province (Henan 2001:p.802, fig.541.3, colour pls.21.2 and 21.3). Despite of the heavily rusted surface on the present piece, we can still see some traces of line decoration which could have been X or inverted V-shaped designs, not dissimilar to those found on the li above.

1.河南省文物考古研究所《鄭州商城》（中）第802頁，圖五四一‧3，（下）彩版二一‧2、3，文物出版社2001年版。

6

獸面紋觚

商代早期（公元前16世紀－前15世紀中葉）

高15.5厘米　口徑9.9厘米　腹深11厘米　腹徑5.3厘米　重279克

這件獸面紋觚口略侈，斜頸直腹，圈足外撇，圈足有三個較大的等距十字形鏤孔，整體比例屬於商代早期粗矮形的觚。腹下部飾剔地輪廓綫的獸面紋，上下各有三道弦紋。此觚與鄭州銘功路屬於二里岡上層一期文化墓葬中出土的獸面紋觚（MGM2:8）[1]，形制、紋飾均基本相同，應該是同時期的青銅器。

_Gu_ (wine vessel) with animal masks

Early Shang (16th – mid 15th century BC)

Height 15.5cm, diameter of mouth 9.9cm, depth 11cm, diameter of belly 5.3cm, weight 279g

This short _gu_ with animal masks has a trumpet mouth, a slanting neck, a straight belly and a foot-ring with three cruciform perforations. On the lower part of belly is a band of animal masks in raised threads between two groups of bow-string pattern. The vessel bears the same form and decoration as a _gu_ (MGM2:8) unearthed from a burial dating from the first phase of upper Erligang stratum at Minggong Road, Zhengzhou (Henan 2001:p.813, fig.547.6, colour pl.30.2). The two _gu_ should be of the same period.

1.河南省文物考古研究所《鄭州商城》（中）第813頁，圖五四七·6，（下）彩版三〇·2，文物出版社2001年版。

7

鳥 紋 扁 足 鼎

商代中期（公元前15世紀中葉－前13世紀）

高15.5厘米　口徑18.1厘米　腹深7厘米　腹徑16.7厘米　重1406.3克

　　這是件淺腹圓底扁足鼎，口沿、立耳都較寬厚，兩耳三足已作五點式勻稱分佈。三足作卷尾龍形，龍頭上昂，張口托起鼎腹。與前文介紹的商代早期弦紋扁足鼎相比，無論在形制的設計，還是鑄造工藝方面都表現出明顯的發展和成熟。

　　鼎的腹部裝飾有一周三組鳥紋，每組有兩個以鳥首爲中心，輔以綫條狀羽飾的回首鳥紋，上下各有一道空心聯珠紋作界欄。這種鳥紋過去沒有被正確認識，常常被誤稱爲夔龍紋、饕餮紋等。其實儘管這種鳥紋與商代晚期以後的鳥紋相比，尚不具備完整的禽類體軀形象，但以鳥喙爲特徵的鳥首形象還是可以辨認的。這種鳥紋最早約出現在商代早期的青銅器上，在商代中期的青銅器上比較多見，在安陽殷墟一期墓葬出土的青銅器上仍可見到此類鳥紋的裝飾[1]。

　　美國夏威夷火奴魯魯美術學院藏有一件器形、紋飾均與此完全相同的鳥紋扁足鼎[2]，它們很有可能是同一組扁足鼎中的兩件。

Ding (food vessel) with bird pattern and flat legs

Mid Shang (mid 15th – 13th century BC)

Height 15.5cm, diameter of mouth 18.1cm, depth 7cm, diameter of belly 16.7cm, weight 1406.3g

This shallow, round *ding* has two big handles set on an everted thick rim and three legs cast in the shape of dragons with curved tails. The two handles and the three legs are on the cardinal points of a pentagon. Compared with No.4 *ding* in this catalogue, the current vessel displays obvious improvement in the design of form and casting techniques.

Around the belly are decorated with three groups of birds between two bands of linked circles. Each group is made up of two bird heads and stylized bodies. This bird design appeared on early Shang bronzes, and became popular in mid Shang. It was still used on the bronzes of the first phase of the Yin Ruins period unearthed from Anyang. In the past, the motif of this design was often misinterpreted as *kui*-dragon or *taotei* mask. As a matter of fact, the bird can still be readily identified through its head with a beak, in spite of its highly stylized body comparing with the more easily recognized bird patterns of the late Shang (Zhou Ya 1997:p.57).

A *ding* bearing identical shape and decoration as the current vessel is in the collection of the Honolulu Academy of Arts, Hawaii (Robert W. Bagley 1987:p.448, fig.80.2). The two might have been from the same group.

---

1. 周亞《商代中期青銅器上的鳥紋》，《文物》1997年第2期第57頁。
2. Robert W.Bagley, *Shang Ritual Bronzes in the Arthur M.Sackler Collections*, p.448,fig.80.2, Harvard University Press,1987.

35

8

獸面紋鬲

商代中期（公元前15世紀中葉－前13世紀）

高18.3厘米　口徑14.3厘米　腹深10.9厘米　腹徑13.6厘米　重1225.9克

　　小立耳，平沿上有一周唇邊，短頸略斜，腹微鼓出，腹底分襠較淺，空心錐足。頸部飾一周獸面紋，腹部在每兩足間用平行的凸弦紋組成三個三角形，相互連接成通常所謂的人字形弦紋。

　　商代早期的鬲一般頸、腹不分，袋腹較深，所以分襠也比較明顯。稍晚一些的鬲，頸、腹出現分界，腹底分襠變淺，這件獸面紋鬲就是屬於後一種形制的鬲。輝縣琉璃閣110號墓和黃陂盤龍城李家嘴2號墓中各出土一件類似的獸面紋鬲[1]，只是前者的獸面紋是用凸起的細綫條勾勒出來的，後者的獸面紋則是用剔地方法表現出來的。與琉璃閣和盤龍城的獸面紋鬲相比較，這件鬲的器壁略厚，特別是兩耳三足已作五點式分佈，表現出更爲成熟的特點，其年代應晚於它們。

　　《輝縣發掘報告》的作者非常仔細地觀察到琉璃閣出土鬲的腹底有一個舊補痕迹，他詳細地描述到："腹底舊有補釘，腹底的内外各附有一圓形銅片，外部銅片的中央並有一圓柱突起。"展品中獸面紋鬲的腹底相同部位也有一個補釘，這種補釘一般都認爲是在出現鑄造缺陷時才作的補鑄。由於在這兩件鬲的相同部位，以及在其他部分早期青銅器的相同部位，也發現過這種補鑄的痕迹，我們有理由認爲應該重新審視這種補鑄產生的原因，它們究竟是爲了彌補鑄造缺陷，還是爲了彌補因當時合範技術原始而造成的孔洞？如果是前者，那麼又爲什麼總是在此部位會出現鑄造缺陷呢？它們的産生與當時的合範技術又有怎樣的關係呢？這些是我們以後可以探究的問題。

_Li_ (food vessel) with animal masks

Mid Shang (mid 15th – 13th century BC)
Height 18.3cm, diameter of mouth 14.3cm, depth 10.9cm, diameter of belly 13.6cm, weight 1225.9g

This _li_ has two handles standing on an everted and thicked rim, a short neck and a pouch-shaped belly supported by three hollow, conical legs. Its neck is decorated with a band of animal masks and the body with inverted V-shaped design made up of parallel raised lines.

In the early Shang period, the neck and belly of _li_ were connected as a unity, and the belly had a bottom in the shape of three linked deep pouches. Later, the neck and belly were clearly separated and the bottom of belly turned to be shaped as shallow pouches. The current _li_ is such a later example.

Two similar _li_ with animal masks have been excavated respectively from No.110 burial at Liulige, Huixian, Henan Province and No.2 burial at Lijiazui in Panlongcheng, Huangpi,

1.中國科學院考古研究所《輝縣發掘報告》第23頁，科學出版社1956年版；湖北省文物考古研究所《盤龍城——1963～1994年考古發掘報告》（上）第172頁，圖一一四，文物出版社2001年版。

Hubei Province (Zhongguo 1956:p.23; Hubei 2001:vol. 1, p.172, fig.114). The only difference of these two *li* is the execution of the monster face bands. The former is in raised lines, while the latter is in sunken relief ground. Compared with them, this *li* has a thicker wall, and in particular, its two handles and the three legs are set on the cardinal points of a pentagon. Technically it is more mature and and should be produced slightly later.

The author of *Huixian fajue baogao* pointed out that a *li* unearthed from Liulige has a similar old remedial casting at the interior bottom of the belly. This kind of restoration casting can also be found in the same place at the current *li* and some other early bronze vessels. Was this restoration made in order to make good the imperfection of the bronze casting at that time? Or the restoration was for a casting holes resulting from a defect of the composite moulds? Further studies along these lines will provide a more definite answer to this interesting issue.

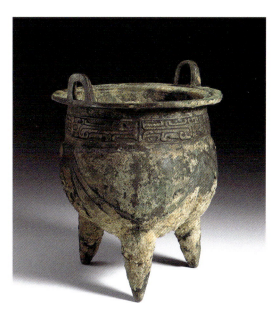

9

圓孔鉞

商代中期（公元前15世紀中葉－前13世紀）
長17.7厘米　寬13.6厘米　內長5.1厘米　內寬3.5厘米　重520.8克

半圓形弧刃，平肩、肩上有兩穿，長方形內位於闌部正中，援部自肩部以下內收與刃部相連，援面有圓形大孔。

這種類型的銅鉞比較少見，在殷墟地區尚未發現。湖北盤龍城楊家灣祭祀坑所出的銅鉞（PYWH6：2）[1]形制與這件相同，時代相當於二里岡上層二期晚段。因此，這件器物的時代應爲商代中期。1964年陝西城固和1979年陝西洋縣出土的商代晚期的虎紋鉞和蛙紋鉞也與此件接近[2]，但在援面的圓形大孔內又飾以鏤空的虎紋和蛙紋。根據考古資料所見，這種類型的銅鉞具有長江流域青銅文化的特點。

***Yue* (axe) with a round hole**

Mid Shang (mid 15th – 13th century BC)
Length 17.7cm, width 13.6cm, length of tang 5.1cm, width of tang 3.5cm, weight 520.8g

Its blade edge is curved in the shape of a semicircle and the flat shoulders are perforatedwith two apertures. The rectangular tang is right in the center of the banister, and there is a large round hole in the middle of the blade.

This type of *yue* is fairly rare and has not been found in the area of Yin Ruins. A *yue* (PYWH6:2), unearthed from a sacrifice pit at Yangjiawan in Panlongcheng, Hubei Province (Hubei 2001:pl.95.2), bears the same shape as this one here, and it can be dated to the late second phase of the upper stratum of the Erligang culture. Thus, this piece should belong to the mid Shang period. A late Shang *yue* with tiger pattern, excavated from Chenggu, Shaanxi Province in 1964, and a *yue* with frog pattern, unearthed from Yangxian, Shaanxi Province in 1979, are similar in shape to this one (Cao Wei 2006:pp.232 and 234); except that the large holes in the blade are decorated with openwork tiger and frog motifs respectively. Based on the information from archaeological finds, this type of *yue* possesses features of the bronze culture in the Yangtze River valley.

1.湖北省文物考古研究所《盤龍城——1963~1994年考古發掘報告》（下）圖版九五·2，文物出版社2001年版。

2.曹瑋《漢中出土商代青銅器》第232、234頁，巴蜀書社2006年版。

10

獸面紋觚　商代晚期（公元前13世紀－前11世紀）

高28.3厘米　口徑16.1厘米　腹深18厘米　腹徑3.7厘米　重1231.5克

　　這是一件製作精美與保存完好的青銅觚。侈口，長頸，腹部略鼓，高圈足外撇。腹部、圈足四等分置棱脊，爲這件觚平添了幾分氣勢。頸部依侈張的弧度飾長條蕉葉紋，猶如盛開的花瓣，下飾一周蛇紋。腹部飾內卷角的分解式獸面紋，圈足上部飾一周俯首的爬行龍紋，下飾曲折角的分解式獸面紋。通體紋飾用平整、規矩、細密的雷紋作地紋，令這件不大的青銅觚紋飾顯得繁縟華麗、層次豐富。

***Gu* (wine vessel) with animal masks**

Late Shang (13th – 11th century BC)
Height 28.3cm, diameter of mouth 16.1cm, depth 18cm, diameter of belly 3.7cm, weight 1231.5g

The exquisite and well preserved *gu* has a trumpet mouth, a long neck, a bulging belly and a high flaring foot-ring. The belly and foot are equally separated by four flanges, and this gives the vessel a sense of monumentality. The neck is decorated with plantain leaves above a band of serpents. The belly is cast with stylized animal masks with inward turning horns. On the foot there are two bands of designs: the upper is crawling dragons; the lower is animal masks with angular horns. All the above decorations are reserved against a ground of fine *leiwen* pattern.

11

四瓣目紋觚　　商代晚期（公元前13世紀–前11世紀）

高14.4厘米　口徑10.9厘米　腹深11.5厘米　腹徑5.3厘米　重453.6克

　　觚從比例來看屬於粗矮型的，侈口，斜頸，腹部略鼓，圈足。頸部飾由尾部相連的鳥紋構成的蕉葉紋，下連一周雲紋，腹部飾四瓣目紋，腹與圈足之間有兩道弦紋，圈足飾利爪前伸的鳥紋。用四瓣目紋作爲觚形器的主題紋飾，並不多見，此爲比較特殊的一例。安陽殷墟西區793號墓出土有一件腹部裝飾有四瓣目紋的觚，器形、尺寸都與此觚比較相似[1]。英國牛津大學阿斯莫利博物館也收藏有一件與此幾乎完全相同的四瓣目紋觚[2]。

　　觚的腹下部對稱地各有一個未鏤空的十字形，這應該是常見於商代青銅器圈足上鏤空十字孔的一種遺存現象。與一般觚形器的腹底，在圈足十字孔之上的做法不同，這件觚的腹底在這兩個未鏤空的十字形之下。如此，從外形上說，腹部下面有兩道弦紋的部位仍是腹部，而不是圈足部分，從而形成了一段假圈足的現象。

***Gu* (wine vessel) with pattern of eyes on quatrefoils**

Late Shang (13th – 11th century BC)
Height 14.4cm, diameter of mouth 10.9cm, depth 11.5cm, diameter of belly 5.3cm, weight 453.6g

Somewhat thicker and shorter than the normal *gu*, this vessel has a trumpet mouth, a long neck, a bulging belly and a foot-ring. Around its neck are plantain leaves containing stylized bird pattern, above a band of clouds. The belly is decorated with eyes on quatrefoils, and the foot with birds with sharp claws; between them are two bow-strings.

It is rare to find such a *gu* with designs of eyes on quatrefoils as the main motif. A *gu* bearing similar decoration, form and size was unearthed from the burial M793 in the west part of the Yin Ruins, Anyang, Henan Province (Zhongguo 1979:p.27, pl.13.3). An almost identical *gu* with also eyes on quatrefoils is in the collection of the Ashmolean Museum, the University of Oxford (Minao Hayashi 1984. p.318; and for details of the design, see Minao Hayashi 1986:p.323, fig.12-107).

There are two crosses symmetrically arranged around the lower belly, which differs from the cruciform perforations seen on the foot-ring of usual Shang bronzes. The bottom of the belly in other *gu* vessels is normally above the perforations, while this *gu*'s base is beneath the crosses. So the part of surface decorated with two bow-strings still belongs to the belly, not the foot.

1.中國社會科學院考古研究所《1969–1977年殷墟西區墓葬發掘報告》，《考古學報》1979年第1期第27頁，圖版十三·3。報告中稱此觚腹部紋飾爲饕餮紋，因圖版不清，無法細辨。對此觚紋飾的再認識，是岳洪彬在其《殷墟青銅禮器研究》一書第230頁中提及的。

2.林巳奈夫《殷周時代青銅器之研究·殷周青銅器綜覽一·圖版》第318頁之觚18，吉川弘文館1984年版。紋飾的細圖可參閱林巳奈夫《殷周時代青銅器之研究·殷周青銅器綜覽二》第323頁12–107圖，吉川弘文館1986年版。

12

父乙觶

商代晚期（公元前13世紀–前11世紀）

高10.4厘米　口橫7.85厘米　口縱6.8厘米　腹深8.3厘米　腹徑8.3厘米　重415.8克

　　侈口，口沿爲圓角長方形，束頸，腹部微鼓，最大徑在腹部偏下，圈足較高略外撇。口沿下飾內卷角的獸面紋，獸面分解，淺浮雕。腹部飾分解式獸面紋，雙目特巨，鼻子突出，鼻頭特大。圈足飾相對的兩組龍紋，器內底鑄銘文兩行3字：

父乙。

　　1962年河南安陽大司空村南53號墓出土殷墟四期的母乙觶[1]與此件形制、紋飾完全一致，但是母乙觶有器蓋。從考古資料看，這種橢方形觶出土時大多都是有器蓋的，估計此器也應有蓋，今已遺失。　父乙觶的紋飾風格很有特色，整個面部輪廓突出器表，極爲醒目。北京保利藝術博物館所藏的一件神面卣[2]，其風格也與這件父乙觶有異曲同工之妙。

***Zhi* (wine vessel) with inscription '*fu yi*'**

Late Shang (13th – 11th century BC)

Height 10.4cm, length of mouth 7.85cm, width of mouth 6.8cm, depth 8.3cm, diameter of belly 8.3cm, weight 415.8g

The *zhi* has a wide mouth, a contracted neck, a bulging belly, a flaring foot-ring and an ovoid section. On the exterior and below the rim is a band of dislocated animal masks with inward curved horns in relief. The belly is also decorated with animal masks with big eyes and protruding noses. Along the foot are two groups of dragons. Three characters, '*fu yi*', are cast on the inside base.

A *zhi* with the same form and decoration as the current vessel, but with an inscription of '*mu yi*' and a lid, was unearthed from the burial M53 in the south of Dasikongcun, Anyang, Henan Province (Zhongguo 1964:pl.1.1), which dates from the fourth phase of the Yin Ruins period. Archaeological materials reveal that this kind of oval *zhi* always originally came with a lid. So the current *zhi* must have had a lid which is now lost.

The relief animal mask design on the vessel has a special charm. A *you* bearing animal masks in a similar style is in the collection of the Poly Art Museum, Beijing (Baoli 2001:p.103).

1.中國科學院考古研究所安陽發掘隊《1962年安陽大司空村發掘簡報》，《考古》1964年第8期圖版一·1。

2.保利藏金編輯委員會《保利藏金》第103頁，嶺南美術出版社1999年版。

13

鴞卣

商代晚期（公元前13世紀－前11世紀）

高19.6厘米　口橫11.9厘米　口縱8.9厘米　腹深11厘米　腹橫15.1厘米　腹縱11.4厘米
重1155.7克

　　器形爲兩隻相背而立的鴞形，敞口，鼓腹，四足內空。有蓋，四坡形蓋鈕。蓋爲鴞首，圓眼有神，尖喙下彎。器爲鴞身，雙翅外揚。器兩側有獸首形貫耳，用來穿繩提攜。整器紋飾爲浮雕構成，綫條簡潔疏朗，不施地紋。

　　1957年山西石樓二郎坡出土的鴞卣[1]與此件器物的形制、紋飾完全相同。殷墟地區出土的鴞卣普遍飾以繁密華麗的紋飾，以1980年河南安陽大司空村南539號墓所出的鴞卣爲代表[2]。有些地區雖出有這種紋飾簡潔的鴞卣，但形制略有差異，鴞首的尖喙上翹，器兩側設繩索狀提梁。湖北應城文化館所藏的鴞卣[3]以及上海博物館所藏的徙卣[4]即爲這種特點。

You (wine vessel) in the shape of two owls

Late Shang (13th – 11th century BC)
Height 19.6cm, length of mouth 11.9cm, width of mouth 8.9cm, depth 11cm, length of belly 15.1cm, width of belly 11.4cm, weight 1155.7g

The _you_, taking the form of two owls standing back to back, has a lid topped by a gable roof-shaped knob, a wide mouth, a bulging belly and four hollow legs. The lid is cast like the owls' heads with round eyes and downward short beaks. The belly is in the shape of the owls' body with wings. Each of two sides has an animal mask shape tubular handle. A string can be attached to these handles to carry the vessel. The decoration is in simple relief design, with the background unadorned.

A very similar _you_ was unearthed from Erlangpo, Shilou, Shanxi Province in 1957 (Shanxi 1958: cover plate). Those owl-shaped _you_ found in the Yin Ruins are often decorated with sophisticated and elaborated patterns, such as that from the burial M539 in the south of Dasikongcun, Anyang, Henan Province (Zhongguo 1992:pl.3.1). Owl-shaped _you_ with simple decoration have also been found in other areas, extant examples of which can be found in the Yingcheng Cultural Centre, Hubei Province (Zhongguo Qingtongqi 1998:p.152) and the Shanghai Museum (Chen Peifen 2004:vol.2, p.310), but their shapes are a little different. For example, the beaks of the owls are tilted upward, not downward, and the vessels have overhead horizontal plaited handles instead of two tubular lobes.

1.山西省文管會保管組《山西石樓縣二郎坡出土商周銅器》，《文物參考資料》1958年第1期封面圖版。

2.中國社會科學院考古研究所安陽工作隊《1980年河南安陽大司空村M539發掘簡報》，《考古》1992年第6期圖版三 · 1。

3.中國青銅器全集編輯委員會《中國青銅器全集 · 4》第152頁，文物出版社1998年版。

4.陳佩芬《夏商周青銅器研究》（夏商篇 · 下）第310頁，上海古籍出版社2004年版。

14

乳釘雷紋瓿　商代晚期（公元前13世紀－前11世紀）
高18厘米　口徑16.8厘米　腹深13.2厘米　腹徑29.3厘米　重2271.7克

　　斂口，短頸，肩部外展，腹部鼓張程度較大，內折急收，下承高圈足，圈足上有三個方形大鏤空。頸部飾兩道弦紋，肩部上層飾雲雷紋襯底的變形龍紋，肩部下層飾同向排列的魚紋，乳釘紋作爲眼睛的裝飾凸出器表，腹部飾乳釘雷紋，圈足鏤孔下部飾一周雷紋。

　　這件乳釘雷紋瓿的形制較爲罕見，具有長江流域青銅文化的特點。根據考古資料，殷墟地區出土的瓿多爲圓肩式和折肩式，然而這件器物的形制不見於中原地區。而魚紋又是長江流域青銅器裝飾的一大特色。在殷墟地區的器物中，水器裝飾有魚紋，但不在酒器和食器上裝飾。美國舊金山亞洲藝術博物館收藏的一件乳釘雷紋瓿形制與此相似[1]，唯肩部的三個青蛙浮雕和所飾的變形龍紋，以及圈足所飾的勾連雲紋略有不同。上海博物館所藏的乳釘雷紋瓿也是這種類型[2]，不過其折腹程度更大，乳釘紋更長。這些器物都是長江流域青銅瓿的代表。

Pou (wine vessel) with nipples on a *leiwen* ground

Late Shang (13th – 11th century BC)
Height 18cm, diameter of mouth 16.8cm, depth 13.2cm, diameter of belly 29.3cm, weight 2271.7g

The *pou* has an in-turned mouth, a short neck, a compressed angular profile, a bulging belly and a high foot-ring with three square holes. The neck is decorated with two bow-strings. At the upper shoulder is a design of stylized dragons on a *leiwen* ground. Below it is a band of fish with protruding eyes arranged in the same direction. The belly is cast with nipples and *leiwen* pattern. The latter is also seen on the foot.

The shape of the *pou* is atypical, but is a characteristic of the bronze culture of the Yangtze River valley. It is not seen on the bronzes of Central Plains, especially the area of the Yin Ruins where the bronze *pou* with rounded or angular shoulder were unearthed. In addition, fish is also one of the representative motifs of the bronzes made in the Yangtze River valley. Among the bronze wares discovered in the Yin Ruins, water vessels rather than wine or food vessels are usually decorated with fish. There are two extant objects similar to this *pou* but with different details. One is in the collection of the Asian Art Museum of San Francisco (Zhongguo 1962:p.1122, fig.A795), the other is in the Shanghai Museum (Chen Peifen 2004:vol.2, p.358). All these three vessels are representatives of the bronze *pou* of the Yangtze River valley.

---

1. 中國科學院考古研究所《美帝國主義劫掠的我國殷周銅器集錄》第1122頁A795，科學出版社1962年版。
2. 陳佩芬《夏商周青銅器研究》（夏商篇·下）第358頁，上海古籍出版社2004年版。

52

15

箙榮鼎

商代晚期（公元前13世紀－前11世紀）
高16.1厘米　口徑14厘米　腹深5.3厘米　腹徑12.3厘米　重625.7克

立耳，圓口方唇，腹部較淺，腹壁下收爲圜底，三只龍形扁足外撇，龍口高揚托住鼎底，尾尖上卷。器底有修補痕迹。腹部有六條對稱的扉棱，相隔成六個區間，每個區間飾一條雲雷紋襯底的内卷角龍紋，組成三組獸面紋。扁足上用細紋勾勒出龍身的綫條，雙目鼓出，炯炯有神。腹内壁鑄銘文2字：

葡（箙）熒（榮）。

林巳奈夫先生在其著作中曾記録了一件箙榮鼎[1]，時代被定爲西周早期。根據對器形和銘文的辨認，可以確定正是此件。1984年河南安陽戚家莊東269號墓所出殷墟三期的疋未鼎，其形制、紋飾與這件較爲相似[2]。河南鹿邑太清宫長子口墓所出幾件西周早期的扁足鼎[3]，腹部更淺，裝飾很細的兩周雷紋，其風格相距較遠。由此推論，此器的時代放在商代晚期是比較合適的。箙榮鼎的流傳及收藏情況不詳，資料從未正式發表。

Ding (food vessel) with inscription '*fu rong*'

Late Shang (13th – 11th century BC)
Height 16.1cm, diameter of mouth 14cm, depth 5.3cm, diameter of belly 12.3cm, weight 625.7g

This round, shallow *ding* has two handles rising from the thick lip and three flaring flat legs in the shape of dragons with a curved tail. The bottom has been restored. The exterior is cast with a broad band of six dragons with rolling horns separated by six flanges, forming, in turn, three animal masks. Two characters, '*fu rong*', are cast in the interior.

The collecting history of this vessel is undocumented but Hayashi Minao published this very *ding* in his studies (Minao Hayashi 1984:No.27 *ding* with flat legs) and dated it to the early Western Zhou. After some further research, however, we pre-date this *ding* to the late Shang. A closely related *ding* with an inscription '*pi wei*' and a similar shape and decoration was excavated from the burial M269 at Qijiazhuang, Anyang, Henan Province in 1984 (Anyang 1991:pl.10.4), which has been dated to the third phase of the Yin Ruins period. Although several early Western Zhou *ding* with flat legs have been unearthed from a burial at Changzikou, Taiqinggong, Luyi, Henan Province (Henan 2000:colour pls.19,20 and 21), they all have a shallower belly decorated with two bands of finer *leiwen* patterns, and are obviously in a different style from the Fu Rong *ding*.

1.林巳奈夫《殷周時代青銅器之研究 · 殷周青銅器綜覽一 · 圖版》扁足鼎27，吉川弘文館1984年版。
2.安陽市文物工作隊《殷墟戚家莊東269號墓》，《考古學報》1991年第3期圖版十 · 4。
3.河南省文物考古研究所、周口市文化局《鹿邑太清宫長子口墓》彩版一九、二〇、二一，中州古籍出版社2000年版。

16

舌簋

商代晚期（公元前13世紀－前11世紀）
高13.2厘米　口徑19.1厘米　腹深10.1厘米　腹徑18厘米　重1958.1克

　　無耳，侈口，束頸，腹部外鼓，腹徑略小于口徑，下承高圈足，高圈足上有三個等距離分佈的方形小鏤孔。口沿下飾一周蕉葉紋，內添雲雷紋，上腹部飾雲雷紋襯底的小鳥紋，尖喙，無冠羽，雙翅上翹，兩爪前伸，尾羽爲弧形下垂狀，尾端平齊。浮雕小獸首將紋飾帶間隔爲三個區間，下腹部飾乳釘雷紋，圈足飾雲雷紋襯底的獸面紋。內底有一塊方形的修補痕迹，上面鑄銘文1字：

　　舌。

　　這是作器者的族徽。

　　舌簋上的小鳥紋流行時間不長，在殷墟婦好墓中有所發現，大致限於殷墟二、三期。1976年河南安陽小屯村北18號墓出土殷墟二期的圍侯簋（M18∶5）[1]，其形制、紋飾均與舌簋相同。因此，舌簋的年代下限不會晚於殷墟三期。

　　傳世的"舌"器較多，據傳多出於河南安陽附近。由此推斷，舌族的族居地應在殷墟地區。一位浙江的私人收藏家收藏有一件舌鼎，通高22.9厘米、口徑19厘米、腹深12.2厘米、重4040.4克。直口方唇，上有立耳，深腹圓底，腹壁微微外鼓，下置柱足（插圖1）。口沿下飾三組獸面紋，獸目突出，面部比例較小，雲雷紋爲地紋，腹部飾以乳釘雷紋（插圖2），內底鑄銘文："舌"（插圖3）。舌鼎的風格與舌簋比較接近，當爲同時代的器物。

Gui (food vessel) with inscription '_she_'

Late Shang (13th – 11th century BC)
Height 13.2cm, diameter of mouth 19.1cm, depth 10.1cm, diameter of belly 18cm, weight 1958.1g

The _gui_ has a trumpet mouth, a contracted neck, a bulging belly supported by a high foot-ring with three square holes. Under the rim on the exterior is a band of plantain leaves on a ground of _leiwen_ pattern. Below it is a band of birds with sharp beaks, forward-extended claws, raised wings and drooping arc tails, but no crest, separated by three small animal heads. The belly is cast with the nipples, and the foot-ring with animal masks on a _leiwen_ ground. A pictographic character '_she_' is cast on a square remedial restoration on the interior. _She_ should be the clan badge of the person who commissioned this _gui_.

The bird design of the _gui_, also seen on some bronze wares from the Fuhao's burial of the Yin Ruins, had been used for a short period of time spanning the second and third phases of the Yin Ruins period. A _gui_ with the same shape and decoration, made for Marquis of Wei and dated from the second phase of the Yin Ruins period, was excavated from the burial M18 at Xiaotuncun, Anyang, Henan Province in 1976 (Zhongguo 1981:pl.10.3). So the latest date for this She _gui_ should not be later than the third phase of the Yin Ruins period.

Extant bronze wares with the inscription of _she_ were mainly found at Anyang, Henan Province, so the She people was supposed to live in the same area. A private collector in Zhejiang Province has a She _ding_ (height 22.9cm, diameter of mouth 19cm, depth12.2cm, weight 4040.4g). It has two handles rising from the square lip, a deep belly with a round bottom and three cylindrical legs. Under the lip are three groups of animal masks on a ground of _leiwen_, above nipple patterns in the main part of the belly. A character, '_she_', is likewisely cast in the interior of the _ding_. The vessel is in the same style of the She _gui_, and should be of the same date.

1.中國社會科學院考古研究所安陽工作隊《安陽小屯村北的兩座殷墓》，《考古學報》1981年第4期圖版十‧3。

（插圖1）

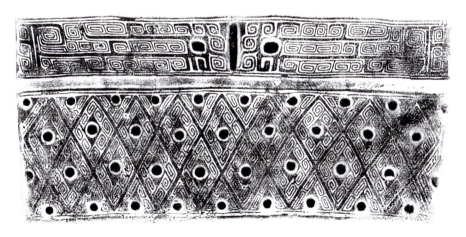

（插圖2）

（插圖3）

17

子廟父丁豆

商代晚期（公元前13世紀－前11世紀）
高9.7厘米　口徑11.15厘米　腹深4.1厘米　腹徑10.1厘米　重386.1克

　　侈口，方折沿，淺盤，微鼓，圜底，高粗柄微外撇。盤腹飾火紋一周，柄部飾兩道弦紋。盤腹內底鑄銘文4字：

　　子廟父丁。

　　傳世的子廟器較多，清宮原舊藏有一件子廟父丁卣[1]，今此器已不知下落。這件子廟父丁豆與商代晚期龔戲豆的形制、紋飾十分相同[2]，但龔戲豆的柄部沒有二道弦紋。1987年河南安陽郭家莊東南1號墓出有殷墟四期的弦紋豆[3]與子廟父丁豆的形制也較相似，弦紋豆的體形較寬，深盤，盤腹有二道弦紋。因此，子廟父丁豆的時代應屬於商代晚期。

　　根據目前的發現，商代晚期出土的銅豆很少，陶豆、木豆的資料比較豐富。河南安陽郭家莊1號墓出土的是殷墟地區唯一一件商代晚期的銅豆，其他均出土於殷墟以外的地區。此時的銅豆具有比較明顯的地方特色。

Dou **(food vessel)**
with inscription
'*zi zhi fu ding*'

Late Shang (13th – 11th century BC)
Height 9.7cm, diameter of mouth 11.15cm, depth 4.1cm, diameter of belly 10.1cm, weight 386.1g

The *dou* has a wide mouth with an everted rim, a shallow belly with a round bottom, and a slightly flaring stem foot. The exterior of the wall is cast with fire patterns, and the stem with two bow-string lines. A four-character inscription, '*zi zhi fu ding*', is cast in the interior, indicating Zizhi commissioned this *dou* in memory of his deceased father Ding.

Many vessels with the inscription of *zi zhi* can be seen today. A bronze *you* cast with *zi zhi fu ding* was included in the former Qing imperial collection (*Xi Qing Gu Jian*, 15.3), but is lost now. This *dou*'s shape and decoration resemble those of a *dou* with inscription 龔戲 of the late Shang (Cheng Changxin 1982:pl.6.5), while the latter does not have two bow-strings at its stem. Another comparable vessel is a broad *dou* with bow-string pattern, which is dated to the fourth phase of the Yin Ruins period. It was unearthed from the burial M1, Guojiazhuang, Anyang, Henan Province in 1987 (Zhongguo 1988:pl.3.2). Thus, the present *dou* inscribed '*zi zhi fu ding*' should be cast in the late Shang.

Only a few bronze *dou* of the late Shang have been found in archaeological excavations so far, but pottery and wooden ones are plentiful. The bronze *dou* from Anyang mentioned above is the only one unearthed from the Yin Ruins area. All the other bronze *dou* were discovered in other areas and are with distinct provincial features.

1.《西清古鑒》15‧3
2.程長新等《北京揀選一組二十八件商代帶銘銅器》，《文物》1982年第9期圖版六‧5。
3.中國社會科學院考古研究所安陽工作隊《1987年夏安陽郭家莊東南殷墓的發掘》，《考古》1988年第10期圖版三‧2。

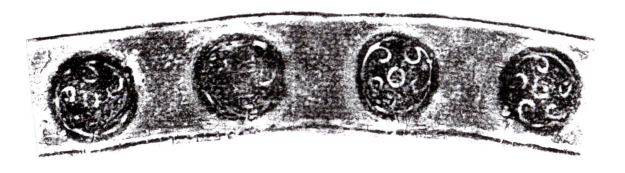

18

瞿冊盤

商代晚期（公元前13世紀－前11世紀）

高10.8厘米　口徑28.8厘米　腹深6.35厘米　腹徑25.2厘米　重2023.6克

　　無耳，侈口，寬沿，腹壁圓轉內收，高圈足微外撇，無折沿。腹部飾一周斜角雲目紋，外底有網狀綫。斜角雲目紋是殷墟銅器上常見的紋飾之一，一般用作輔助紋飾。殷墟二期則以相對較寬的帶狀形式作爲主體紋飾使用。腹內底鑄銘文2字：

　　瞿冊。

　　是"瞿"族擔任過作冊這個官職。

　　這件瞿冊盤曾見於著録[1]，時代被定爲西周早期。從器物形制看，瞿冊盤是無耳盤，沒有出現扉棱，圈足也未出現折沿，這些均顯示出其時代並不會太晚。而且高圈足，以及腹部所飾的斜角雲目紋等特徵，與殷墟二期婦好墓所出的銅盤[2]有相似之處。由此可見，瞿冊盤的時代不宜過晚，歸入商代晚期是適當的。此外，《殷周金文集成》所收其他瞿冊器的時代均定商代[3]，這不失爲一個旁證。

Pan (water vessel) with inscription 'ju ce'

Late Shang (13th – 11th century BC)
Height 10.8cm, diameter of mouth 28.8cm, depth 6.35cm, diameter of belly 25.2cm, weight 2023.6g

This shallow *pan* has an everted rim and a high foot-ring. Under the rim on the exterior is a band of cloud eyes and on the base is a net pattern. As one of common decorations on the bronzes unearthed from the Yin Ruins, the cloud eyes were mainly used as supplementary designs. On the bronzes of the 2nd phase of the Yin Ruins period, however, the cloud eyes in the form of a broad band functions as the primary decorative design. Two characters, '*ju ce*', cast in the interior indicate that the Ju people was appointed as *zuoce*, an official post.

This *pan* has been published and has been previously dated to the early Western Zhou (Minao Hayashi1984:No.33 pan). According to our research, as it does not have handles, flanges and an everted foot rim, its date should not be so late. Additionally, its high foot-ring and the pattern of cloud eyes are similar to those of a *pan* discovered in the Fuhao's burial of the Yin Ruins (Zhongguo 1980:pls. 61.2 and 62.2). So we suggest that the *pan* should be dated to the late Shang period instead. This is also supported by *Yin Zhou Jinwen Jicheng* (The Collection of Shang and Zhou Inscriptions) edited by Chinese Institute of Social Science and Archaeology (Zhongguo 2007:vol.7, fig.10030), which dates some bronze objects with inscriptions of *ju ce* to Shang.

1.林巳奈夫《殷周時代青銅器之研究・殷周青銅器綜覽一・圖版》盤33，吉川弘文館1984年版。

2.中國社會科學院考古研究所《殷墟婦好墓》圖版陸壹・2、陸貳・2，文物出版社1980年版。

3.中國社會科學院考古研究所《殷周金文集成》（第七冊）修補增訂本10030，中華書局2007年版。

19

獸面紋鉞

商代晚期（公元前13世紀－前11世紀）

長17.4厘米　寬10.9厘米　內長6.1厘米　內寬4.9厘米　重284.7克

　　弧刃，平肩，長方形內不在闌部正中，構成上肩窄，下肩寬，援部由肩部向刃部逐漸外侈，亦呈現出援部上側短、下側長的特徵。內端和援部後端均飾虎耳獸面紋。紋飾是用綫條勾勒出輪廓，估計原先內有填充物，今已脫落。援部後端的獸面紋爲正反兩面折叠式，一面只爲半個獸面形狀。

　　這種類型的銅鉞，主要流行於商至西周，春秋以後罕見。其時代變化的特點是由較窄而長，向寬扁發展，刃角向上翹起的幅度漸大。1986年河南安陽大司空村南地25號墓出土殷墟二期的銅鉞（M25:15）[1]與這件獸面紋鉞形制、紋飾相同，但其內上有一穿，有利於更好的固定木柄。獸面紋鉞的時代當與此相近。

Yue (axe) with animal masks

Late Shang (13th – 11th century BC)

Length 17.4cm, width 10.9cm, length of tang 6.1cm, width of tang 4.9cm, weight 284.7g

The blade edge of this _yue_ is curved and the shoulders are flattened. The rectangular tang is not set in the center of the banister, which makes the shoulders not symmetrical, the upper one narrower than the lower. The tang and the lower part of blade are both decorated with animal masks with tiger ears delineated with sunken lines originally filled in with some material which is now all gone.

This type of bronze _yue_ was popular during the Shang and Western Zhou dynasties and was rarely found after the Spring and Autumn period. Its shape, as time went by, changed from being narrow and long to being wide and flat, and the edge angle of the blade gradually increased. A _yue_ (M25:15), excavated from the burial M25 in the south of Dasikongcun, Anyang, Henan Province (Zhongguo 1989:pl.4.2) and dated to the second phase of Yin Ruins period, is similar to this one both in the shape and decoration. The only difference is an aperture in the tang for hafting a wooden shaft. This _yue_ with animal masks can be dated to almost the same period as M25 _yue_.

1.中國社會科學院考古研究所安陽工作隊《1986年安陽大司空村南地的兩座殷墓》，《考古》1989年第7期圖版肆·2。

20

夷 爵　西周早期（公元前11世紀）
高20.7厘米　流至尾16.7厘米　腹深9.4厘米　腹徑6厘米　重824.9克

　　短流上揚，尖尾較長，口沿內側靠近鋬部有菌狀柱，獸首形鋬，雙柱較高，距流折已稍遠，腹爲直筒狀，深腹，卵形底，刀形足，足形較寬，三足外撇。腹飾兩道弦紋，柱頂爲火紋，鋬一側柱上及口沿下鑄銘文7字：

尸（夷）乍（作）

父癸寶

尊彝。

　　傳世昭王時期的銅器作册睘卣、作册睘尊[1]，以及1981年陝西扶風强家村1號墓出土的西周中期夷伯簋[2]，銘文中均提到了“夷伯”。夷爵與夷伯簋當爲同一國族，即夷國族。
　　這件夷爵的形制具有西周早期銅爵的典型特徵。1967年長安張家坡80號墓出土西周成康時期的◫爵（M80∶1）[3]與這件形制、紋飾完全相同。西周早期，酒器開始衰落，銅爵大量減少，其造型風格繼承了殷墟晚期樸素的傳統。

**_Jue_ (wine vessel)
made for Yi**

Early Western Zhou (11th century BC)
Height 20.7cm, overall length 16.7cm, depth 9.4cm, diameter of belly 6cm, weight 824.9g

This vessel has a short spout, a long and pointed tail, two mushroom-shaped high pillars and a handle with animal head. Its body is in a cylindrical shape with a deep belly, a convex bottom and three knife-shaped feet. The belly is decorated with the pattern of two bow strings while the pillar's top with a flaming whorl. The part under the rim and on the pillar bears a seven-character inscription, indicating the _jue_ was made for Yi in memory of his deceased father Kui. _Yibo_ is seen in the inscription on the Zuo Ce Qiong _you_ and the Zuo Ce Qiong _zun_, heirloom bronzes from the period of King Zhao (Wang Shimin 1999:p116 and 126), as well as a _gui_ made for Yibo, found at burial M1 at Qiangjiacun in Fufeng, Shaanxi Province in 1981 (Zhouyuan 1987:p.5). This _jue_ made for Yi and the _gui_ made for Yibo belong to the same Yi State clan.

This _jue_ possesses typical features of the early Western Zhou. A ◫ _jue_ of the period from King Kang to King Cheng, Western Zhou, unearthed from the burial M80 at Zhangjiapo, Chang'an in 1967 has the same shape and decorative pattern as this one (Zhongguo 1980b:fig.36.5). From early Western Zhou onwards wine vessels gradually declined and the number of _jue_ decreased. The few crude surviving ones all inherited the simple decorative style of the late Yin Ruins period.

1. 王世民等《西周青銅器分期斷代研究》第116、126頁，文物出版社1999年版。
2. 周原扶風文管所《陝西扶風强家一號西周墓》，《文博》1987年第4期第5頁。
3. 中國社會科學院考古研究所灃西發掘隊《1967年長安張家坡西周墓葬的發掘》，《考古學報》1980年第4期圖三六·5。

21

南姬爵

西周早期（公元前11世紀）

甲：高23.5厘米　流至口18.6厘米　腹深9.8厘米　腹徑6.6厘米　重1186.4克

乙：高23.6厘米　流至口18.6厘米　腹深10厘米　腹徑6.7厘米　重1325克

這一對銅爵，大小、造型、紋飾皆相同。流口短而寬厚，上揚，短尾上翹，口沿內側靠近鋬部有高傘狀柱，獸首鋬與器體爲二次澆鑄，腹部爲直筒狀，卵形底，三刀形足外撇。流下飾顧龍紋，口沿下飾蕉葉紋，腹部飾獸面紋，流、尾下至腹部有扉棱，棱脊的前端鉤狀內彎。甲件的柱和鋬下鑄銘文5字：

南姬

公寶彝。

乙件的柱和鋬下鑄銘文6字：

南姬

乍（作）公寶彝。

其中，甲件的"作"字全部被鋬壓住，而乙件的"作"字被鋬壓住了上半部，只存留了下半部。可見，這兩件爵的鋬與器體應爲二次鑄造。

西周早期酒器式微，一些器物的裝飾繼承了殷墟晚期樸素的發展方向，還有一些在棱脊裝飾上進一步發展，形成了獨具特色的鉤狀棱脊。南姬爵的流與尾下裝飾的鉤狀棱脊，雖不如何尊那麼華麗，但仍呈現出西周早期青銅器裝飾的一種新風格。

A pair of *Jue* (wine vessel) made for Nanji

Early Western Zhou (11ᵗʰ century BC)

A:height 23.5cm, overall length 18.6cm, depth 9.8cm, diameter of belly 6.6cm, weight 1186.4g

B:height 23.6cm, overall length 18.6cm, depth 10cm, diameter of belly 6.7cm, weight 1325g

These two *jue*, each with short spout and tail as well as umbrella-shaped pillar and animal-headed handle, bear exactly the same size, shape, and decoration. The body is in a cylindrical shape with a convex bottom standing on three knife-shaped feet. The area under the spout is decorated with a head-turning dragon; the part below the rim is decorated with plantain leaves and the belly with animal masks. Along the spout, tail and belly are flanges. An inscription indicating that Nanji commissioned the pair of *jue* in memory of Gong is cast below the pillar of each *jue*. On *jue* A it reads 'Nanji gong bao yi' as the character 'zuo' is covered by its handle. For *jue* B the 'zuo' is readable though only the lower part can be seen, and the six-character inscription reads 'Nanji zuo gong bao yi'. This shows that the handle and the body were cast separately. A precast handle was placed in the clay mould for the casting of such a *jue*.

Wine vessels declined in early Western Zhou. Some vessels continued the late Shang tradition of simple decorative style but there was a new bronze style with heavy flanged ridges, often with hooks. This pair of *jue*, although not as magnificent as the famous He *zun*, still presents some of the flamboyant elements of this innovative decoration style of the early Western Zhou.

甲（左）乙（右）

甲

乙

22

鳶觚

西周早期（公元前11世紀）

高22.2厘米　口徑13.9厘米　腹深16.2厘米　腹徑5.3厘米　重913克

　　敞口，長頸，頸、腹均較粗，腹部微鼓，腹壁弧度較小，高圈足外撇，圈足下有一周較矮的折沿。腹部飾曲折角獸面紋，紋飾突出器表，獸面無輪廓，軀體分解，不施地紋。獸面紋上下分飾二道弦紋。圈足內壁鑄銘文兩行6字：

鳶乍（作）父癸

尊彝。

是鳶爲父癸所作之器。

　　鳶觚是細體觚中較粗的一種類型，所見甚少。殷墟四期粗體觚和平腹觚的復興，對觚的形制發展產生較大影響。這件觚的器壁較厚，裝飾極爲樸素的特點與河南鹿邑太清宮長子口墓所出西周早期的銅觚（M1：83、M1：132）幾乎相同[1]。鳶觚與後述的鳶觶和鳶簋應爲同一人作器。根據鳶觶的銘文推斷，鳶觚的時代應爲西周早期。

_Gu_ (wine vessel) made for 鳶

Early Western Zhou (11th century BC)

Height 22.2cm, diameter of mouth 13.9cm, depth 16.2cm, diameter of belly 5.3cm, weight 913g

The _gu_ has a trumpet mouth, a long neck, a slightly bulging belly, and a high foot-ring with an everted thickened rim. On the belly is decorated with animal masks with angular horns in low relief and between two bow-strings. A six-character inscription cast inside the foot-ring indicates that 鳶 commissioned the _gu_ in memory of his deceased father Kui.

This vessel, as one of the _gu_ with slender profile, is rare for its thicker and somewhat compressed body. Its thick wall and simple decoration are also seen on a few early Western Zhou _gu_ (M1:83 and M1:132) found in the burials at Changzikou, Taiqinggong, Luyi, Henan Province (Henan 2000: colour pl.37). It was made for the same person who commissioned the 鳶 _zhi and the_ 鳶 _gu_ mentioned later in this catalogue. Thus, the _gu_ should be dated from the early Western Zhou period according to the inscription on 鳶 _zhi_.

1.河南省文物考古研究所、周口市文化局《鹿邑太清宮長子口墓》彩版三七，中州古籍出版社2000年版。

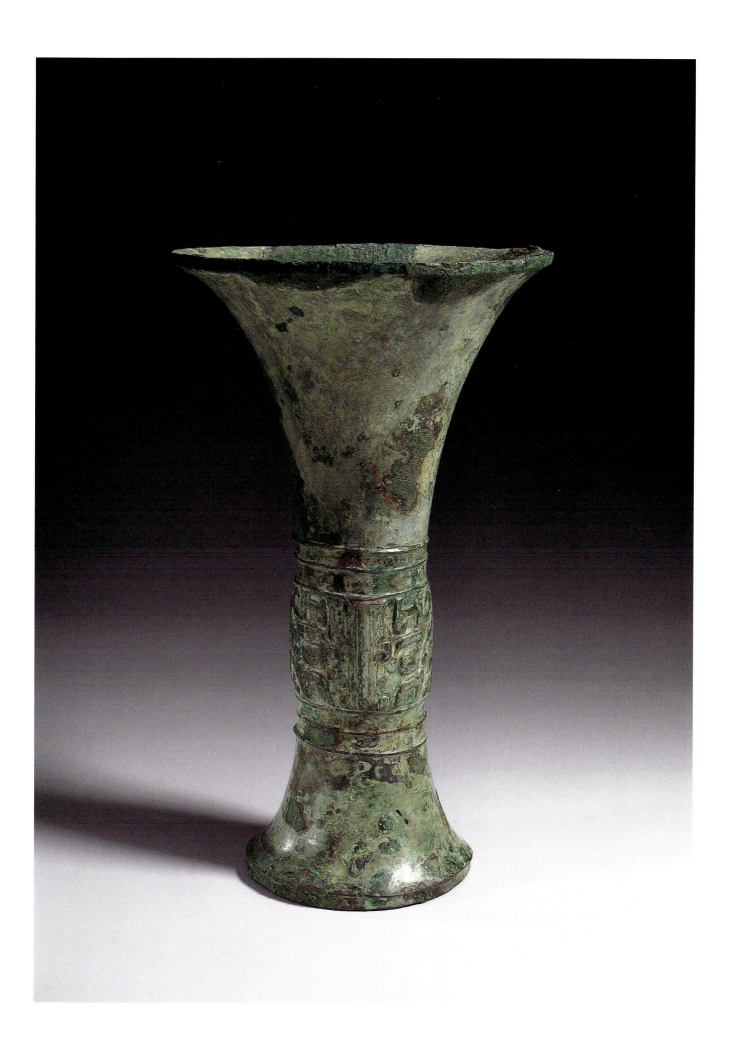

23

奮觶

西周早期（公元前11世紀）

高18.8厘米　口橫11.3厘米　口縱9.1厘米　腹深12厘米　腹徑11.4厘米　重867.3克

器呈橢圓形，有蓋，斂口，束頸，短領，腹部較深，腹壁外鼓，圈足較高，底部外撇成矮階狀，蓋頂爲半環形捉手。蓋沿及腹部飾獸面紋，僅獸目可辨，軀體盡轉化爲雲雷紋，圈足飾斜角雲目紋，蓋和器鑄銘文四行20字：

佳（唯）伯初令（命）于

宗周史奮

易（賜）馬二匹用乍（作）

父癸寶尊彝。

這件奮觶與1974年北京琉璃河251號墓出土西周早期公仲觶（M251：9）[1]的形制完全相同。公仲觶蓋面和頸部飾雲雷紋及連珠紋，圈足飾斜角雲目紋。銅觶出現於商代晚期，西周早期酒器大量減少，但銅觶的數量却有所上升，在出土數據中觶往往替代了觚，與爵形成組合。西周中期以後，觶與大多數酒器一樣，也逐漸退出了青銅器發展的序列。

***Zhi* (wine vessel)
made for 奮**

Early Western Zhou (11th century BC)

Height 18.8cm, length of mouth 11.3cm, width of mouth 9.1cm, depth 12cm,
diameter of belly 11.4cm, weight 867.3g

This lidded and high-footed vessel has an oval section body with a slightly flared mouth, short and contracted neck, a deep belly and a flared bottom. Its lid knob is in semicircular shape. The lid and the belly are cast with animal mask borders; only the eyes of animal are discernible, while the bodies of animal are highly stylized into *leiwen* pattern. The foot-ring is decorated with cloud eyes pattern. The lid and body are cast with a twenty-character inscription in four columns, indicating that 奮 commissioned the *zhi* in memory of his father Kui.

蓋銘　　　　　　　　　　　器銘

This vessel bears the same shape as the Gong Zhong *zhi* (M251:9) of early Western Zhou, unearthed from the burial M251 in Liulihe, Beijing in 1974 (Beijing 1995:pl.65.3). The latter's lid and neck are cast with *leiwen* pattern as well as circle-bordered medallion, and its foot-ring with cloud eyes. Bronze *zhi* appeared during late Shang dynasty. When it came to early Western Zhou, drinking vessels began to decrease in number while the number of bronze *zhi* increased. Among the excavated vessels of late Shang, a large quantity of *zhi*, instead of *gu*, are found together with *jue*. After mid Western Zhou period, *zhi*, like other drinking vessels, gradually faded out of the scene.

1.北京市文物研究所《琉璃河西周燕國墓地1973-1977》圖版六五・3，文物出版社1995年版。

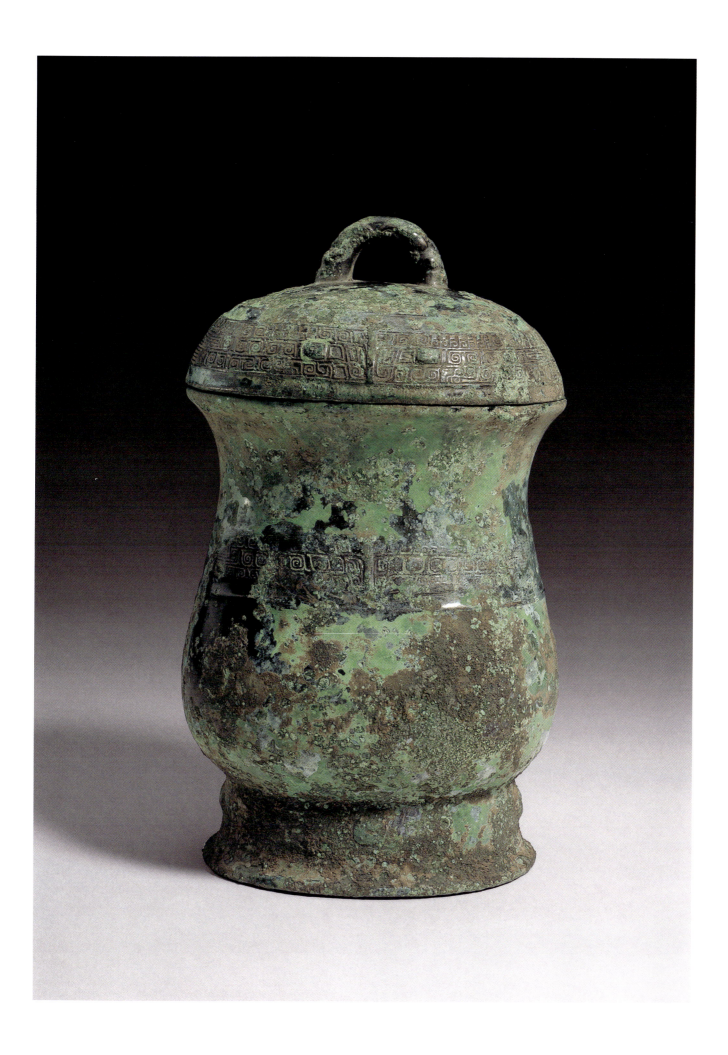

24

牛卣

西周早期（公元前11世紀）

高26.9厘米　口橫11.8厘米　口縱10.7厘米　腹深15.9厘米　腹徑16.2厘米　重3156克

　　器呈橢圓形，直口高蓋，蓋折沿較高，腹部鼓出，高圈足外撇有折沿，蓋頂爲花蕾形抓手，自蓋沿至圈足均勻地設置四條扉棱，提梁兩端設獸首。花蕾形抓手上飾蟬紋，蓋面、蓋沿、腹部及圈足飾各種不同的獸面紋，以雲雷紋爲地紋，蓋沿和圈足的獸面紋相同，蓋面爲尖角獸面紋，腹部爲内卷角獸面紋，頸部飾雲雷紋襯底的花冠式顧龍紋。提梁上飾龍紋，外底部有網狀綫，蓋與器鑄銘文1字：

　　牛。

　　是作器者的族徽。

　　傳世的牛器較少，兩件牛鼎分别藏於故宫博物院[1]和美國費城賓夕法尼亞大學博物館[2]。一件牛簋藏於美國舊金山亞洲美術博物館[3]。1935年安陽侯家莊西北崗1004號墓出土的牛方鼎，“牛”字銘文爲一頭牛的形狀[4]，而不是上述諸器的牛首狀銘文。這件牛卣與1976年陝西扶風莊白1號窖藏所出西周早期商卣的形制相近[5]，但是所飾紋飾以及獸首、扉棱皆不相同。牛卣上裝飾樸素的扉棱也是西周早期的一種新氣象。1975年陝西扶風召李村1號墓出土西周早期的伯卣即裝飾有這種風格的扉棱[6]。

1.中國社會科學院考古研究所《殷周金文集成》（第二册）修補增訂本1103，中華書局2007年版。

2.中國社會科學院考古研究所《殷周金文集成》（第二册）修補增訂本1104。

3.中國社會科學院考古研究所《殷周金文集成》（第三册）修補增訂本2973。

4.中國社會科學院考古研究所《殷周金文集成》（第二册）修補增訂本1102。

5.陝西周原考古隊《陝西扶風莊白一號西周青銅器窖藏發掘簡報》，《文物》1978年第3期圖版二·2。

6.羅西章等《陝西扶風縣召李村一號周墓清理簡報》，《文物》1976年第6期第64頁圖八。

You (wine vessel) with inscription *'niu'*

Early Western Zhou (11th century BC)
Height 26.9cm, length of mouth 11.8cm, width of mouth 10.7cm, depth 15.9cm, diameter of belly 16.2cm, weight 3156g

This high-footed vessel with an oval section has an upright mouth, a tall lid, and a swelling belly. On either side of the handle, there is an animal head; four groups of flanges, each in turn, made up of four units are set on the area from the lid rim to foot-ring. On the top of lid, there is a bud-shaped knob, decorated with cicada design. The surface, rim of the lid, the belly and the foot-ring are all decorated with different types of animal masks, with *leiwen* pattern as background. The animal masks on the lid rim are the same as those along the foot-ring. The neck is decorated with corolla-shaped dragons with turning heads, with *leiwen* pattern as background. Dragon pattern is carved on the handle. Net pattern appears on the base and inside the lid as well as in the body; a one-character inscription *'niu'* is cast, which is the clan badge of the person who commissioned the piece.

Very few bronze vessels with the inscription *'niu'* are known. The extant ones include two *ding*, one in the Palace Museum, Beijing (Zhongguo 2007:vol.2 fig.1103) and the other in the University of Pennsylvania Museum, Philadelphia (Zhongguo 2007:vol.2 fig.1104), and a *gui* in the Asian Art Museum of San Francisco (Zhongguo 2007:vol.3 fig.2973). For the square *ding*, unearthed from a burial (M1004) at Xibeigang, Houjiazhuang, Anyang in 1935, the *'niu'* character is represented by an ox, whereas the characters on the vessels mentioned above are all rendered in the form of an ox head (Zhongguo 2007:vol.2 fig.1102). This *you* is similar in shape to the *you* with the inscription *'shang'* of the early Western Zhou, excavated from No.1 hoard at Zhuangbai, Fufeng County, Shaanxi Province in 1976 (Shaanxi 1978a:pl.2.2), but their decoration, animal-head pattern and flanges are different. The simple and crude flanges on this *you* display a new style of the early Western Zhou. Such flanges are also found on the *Bo you* of the early Western Zhou and excavated from the burial M1 from Zhaolicun, Fufeng, Shaanxi Province in 1975 (Luo Xizhang 1976:p.64, fig.8).

器銘 蓋銘

25

山父丁鼎

西周早期（公元前11世紀）
高32.8厘米　口徑27厘米　腹深26.7厘米　腹徑25.7厘米　重8030克

折沿方唇，立耳厚重，腹壁微鼓，最大徑在腹中部，圓底下承三個粗壯的柱足，柱足上粗下細，足根部略粗。口沿下飾內卷角的獸面紋，以雲雷紋爲地紋，獸面與軀體相連，分辨清楚，卷尾上揚，前爪伸出。足根部飾外卷角獸面紋，下有兩道弦紋。獸面中間皆有扉棱。腹內壁鑄銘文3字：

山父丁。

此鼎形近北京琉璃河253號墓所出的堇鼎[1]，紋飾亦十分相似。這座墓葬同出的還有亞臿方鼎、圉方鼎、圉簋等器，是西周早期成、康之際一組重要的銅器群。1967年長安張家坡87號墓出有西周早期的山爵（M87:8）[2]，以及1973年陝西岐山賀家村1號墓出有西周早期的山簋（M1:5）[3]。可以推知，周人滅商後山族主要活動於這個地區。

傳世的山父丁器還有山父丁觶和山父丁觚[4]。着録中僅有拓片，器形無徵，時代都被定爲商代。以形制而論，山父丁鼎與後述的山父丁盤歸入西周早期似乎較爲妥當。因而，這批山父丁器的時代均可定爲西周早期。

Ding (food vessel) with inscription 'shan fu ding'

Early Western Zhou (11th century BC)
Height 32.8cm, diameter of mouth 27cm, depth 26.7cm, diameter of belly 25.7cm, weight 8030g

This vessel has two thick upright handles, a slightly bloated belly and three strong feet. Below the rim are animal masks on a *leiwen* ground. The animal masks are connected with bodies that are clearly depicted with stretching forepaws and raising tails. Animal masks on the feet have flanges and there are two bow strings below. The interior of this *ding* is cast with a three-character inscription '*shan fu ding*'.

This *ding*'s shape and decoration are quite similar to a *ding* with the inscription '*qin*', unearthed from a burial (M253) in Liulihe near Beijing (Beijing 1995:pl.52). Together with the Qin *ding*, other objects such as a square Yu *ding* and a Yu *gui* are excavated; all of them are regarded as important bronzes from King Cheng and King Kang's reigns of the early Western Zhou. With the findings of early Western Zhou bronzes including a Shan *jue* (M87:8) from a burial (M87) in Zhangjiapo, Chang'an in 1967 (Zhongguo 1980:p.468, fig.16.6) and a Shan *gui* (M1:5) from Qijiacun, Qishan, Shaanxi in 1973 (Shaanxi 1976:p.34, fig.5.4), it can be concluded that the Shan clan stayed in these areas after the Shang regime was overthrown by the Zhou people.

Published bronzes with the inscription of *shan fu ding* include a *zhi* and a *gu* (Zhongguo 2007:vol.5, figs.6261, 7115, 7116, and 7117). Both pieces are dated to the Shang period in the publication, but no illustration is provided except rubbings of the inscriptions. Judging by the form, this *ding* and a *pan* with the inscription of *shan fu ding* should be dated to the early Western Zhou. Thus, all bronzes inscribed with '*shan fu ding*' should be of the early Western Zhou period.

1. 北京市文物研究所《琉璃河西周燕國墓地1973-1977》圖版五二，文物出版社1995年版。
2. 中國社會科學院考古研究所灃西發掘隊《1967年長安張家坡西周墓葬的發掘》，《考古學報》1980年第4期第468頁圖十六·6。
3. 陝西省博物館、陝西省文物管理委員會《陝西岐山賀家村西周墓葬》，《考古》1976年第1期第34頁圖五·4。
4. 中國社會科學院考古研究所《殷周金文集成》（第五冊）修補增訂本6261、7115、7116、7117，中華書局2007年版。

26

夐簋 西周早期（公元前11世紀）

高15.1厘米　口徑20.4厘米　腹深12.2厘米　腹徑22厘米　重3292.8克

　　侈口，束頸，鼓腹，獸首形附耳下有小鉤狀垂珥，高圈足外侈有折沿。頸部和圈足飾獸面紋，以雲雷紋爲地紋，頸部中間設高浮雕的虎耳小獸首，腹內底鑄銘文四行30字：

　　佳（唯）九月者子具服

　　公迺令（命）才（在）庠曰凡

　　朕（朕）臣與晦夐敢

　　對公休用乍（作）父癸寶尊彝。

　　這件器物的紋飾極爲簡單，一掃商末繁縟的紋飾風格，采取了比較簡潔的方式，僅在口沿下及圈足各飾一周紋飾。夐簋與成王時期的禽簋在形制以及紋飾風格上都很類似。但是禽簋的獸首耳下是方形垂珥與此略有不同。

　　夐簋與第23夐觚、第23夐觶，器主爲同一人。

Gui (food vessel) made for 夐

Early Western Zhou (11th century BC)
Height 15.1cm, diameter of mouth 20.4cm, depth 12.2cm, diameter of belly 22cm, weight 3292.8g

This high-footed vessel has a slightly trumpet mouth, a controated neck, a bulging belly and two looped handles with animal heads. Below each handle, there is a lug in the shape of a small hook. Its neck and foot-ring are cast with animal masks on a _leiwen_ ground, and in the middle of the neck are tiger-eared animal heads in high relief. A thirty-character inscription in four columns is cast on the interior, indicating that the vessel was made for 夐 in memory of his deceased father Kui.

The simple decoration of this vessel, very different from the crowded decoration style of the late Shang, highlights only the rim and the foot-ring. This _gui_ is rather similar to a _gui_ with the inscription '_qin_' of the King Cheng period with respect to the shape and decorative style. The only difference between the two vessels is that the Qin _gui_ has square lugs below the handles.

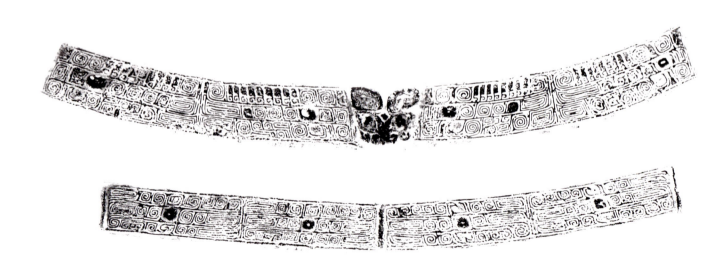

27

山父丁盤　西周早期（公元前11世紀）
高14.7厘米　口徑39厘米　腹深6.9厘米　重4957.6克

　　無耳，口沿較寬，腹部較淺，腹壁圓轉內收，下承高圈足，圈足有高折沿。腹部飾雲雷紋襯底的長鼻龍紋，上下各有一圈連珠紋，圈足飾雲雷紋襯底的顧首鳥紋，上下各有一圈連珠紋，外底部飾有大小兩條龍紋，內底鑄銘文3字：

　　山父丁。

　　山父丁盤與山父丁鼎爲同組器，這種形制的盤最早出現在商代晚期，所見不多。以1990年河南安陽郭家莊160號墓出土的銅盤（M160：97）爲代表[1]。直到西周早期，這種形制仍很少見。河南鹿邑太清宮長子口墓所出的銅盤（M1：210）具有這種特點[2]，此墓的時代一般定爲西周早期，不晚於成王時期。外底部飾紋最早出現在商代晚期，西周時期還有相當多的青銅器外底部亦有飾紋，春秋以後其數量逐漸減少，它是商周時期鑄造工藝發展的見證。

Pan (water vessel) with inscription 'shan fu ding'

Early Western Zhou (11th century BC)
Height 14.7cm, diameter of mouth 39cm, depth 6.9cm, weight 4957.6g

This *pan* has a shallow bowl and a high foot with a flange. The body is decorated with long-nosed dragons on a *leiwen* ground within two rings of beads, which appear again on the foot-ring enclosing birds on a *leiwen* ground. The base is incised with two dragons, one is big and the other is small. A three-character inscription, '*shan fu ding*', is cast in the interior.

Pan and *ding* with the inscription of *shan fu ding* are always found together. *Pan* in this shape first appeared in late Shang and among the rarely known examples is the most representative one (M160:97), excavated from a burial (M160) in Guojiazhuang, Anyang, Henan Province in 1990 (Zhongguo 1998: colour pl.13.1). It was still not popular in the early Western Zhou period. A *pan* unearthed from the Changzikou burial at Taiqing Palace in Luyi County, Henan Province, possesses the features of this present example (Henan 2000:pl. 62.1). The Changzikou burial is generally dated to the early Western Zhou period, not later than King Cheng's reign. Designs engraved on the bottom first appeared on the bronzes of the late Shang period and became popular in the Western Zhou period; the popularity waned since the Spring and Autumn period. This kind of design is a testimony to the development of casting technology in the Shang and Zhou periods.

1.中國社會科學院考古研究所《安陽殷墟郭家莊商代墓葬1982–1992年考古發掘報告》彩版一三·1，中國大百科全書出版社1998年版。

2.河南省文物考古研究所、周口市文化局《鹿邑太清宮長子口墓》彩版六二·1，中州古籍出版社2000年版。

28

父丁母丁戈　西周早期（公元前11世紀）
長32.9厘米　援長23.3厘米　闌長7.9厘米　重383.3克

　　長條形援，援上有柳葉形脊，援下刃下延成微胡，胡上一穿，有上下闌，內上無穿，內前端位於援本上部，內上援與援上刃連爲一綫，內後端的正面作立鳥形，勾喙較長，向內彎曲，歧冠向外伸出，鳥首後側有彎角，鳥的身尾較短且向上彎曲，內的一面鑄銘文4字：

　　父丁母丁。

　　戈上裝秘後，內上的銘文爲倒書，這種現象是有銘戈的一種常制。
　　曲內戈流行時間不長，至西周早期已經極爲少見。商代晚期的歧冠式曲內戈還未出現微胡，而這件戈的形制與1974年北京琉璃河205號墓所出西周早期的戈（M205:6）極爲相似[1]。究其原因，可能是受到了此時最爲流行的直內有胡戈的影響。但是作爲商文化典型代表的曲內戈，進入西周以後自然就很快消亡了。

Ge (dagger-axe) with inscription *'fu ding mu ding'*

Early Western Zhou (11th century BC)
Overall length 32.9cm, length of blade 23.3cm, length of banister 7.9cm, weight 383.3g

This *ge* has a long *yuan* (blade) with a willow-shaped ridge, a small *hu* (dewlap or the lower edge of the blade) with a hole, a *lan* (banister) and a *na* (tang) without holes. The tang takes the form of a standing bird with a long hook beak, a crest, a curved horn and a short tail. A four-character inscription, '*fu ding mu ding*', is cast on the other side of the tang, indicating the *ge* was made for its owner in memory of his deceased parents.

The *ge* with a curved tang was used for a short period of time and came to be very rare by the early Western Zhou. In addition, during the late Shang dynasty, the *ge* with a curved crest-shaped tang did not have a dewlap. This *ge*, however, looks similar to an early Western Zhou *ge* unearthed from the burial M251 at Liulihe, Beijing in 1974 (Beijing 1995:pl.72.1). This discovery shows that there might have been an influence from the *ge* with a straight tang and a dewlap popular in the early Western Zhou. But in any case, the typical *ge* with a curved tang of the Shang culture, disappeared quickly in the Western Zhou dynasty.

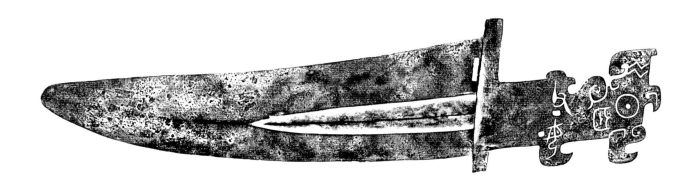

1.北京市文物研究所《琉璃河西周燕國墓地1973-1977》圖版七二‧1，文物出版社1995年版。

29

鳥紋觶 西周中期（公元前11世紀末－前10世紀末）

高12.2厘米　口橫10.6厘米　口縱7.8厘米　腹深10厘米　腹徑10.9厘米　重459.2克

　　器呈橢方形，侈口，束頸，口沿爲圓角長方形，腹部呈傾垂狀，最大徑靠近腹底，矮圈足底部外撇。頸部飾一周雲雷紋襯底的分尾鳥紋，尖喙，頭上有綬帶式冠羽，雙翅上翹，尾羽分爲兩段，上一段向後延伸，下一段前端向下卷，後端向上卷，呈橫的S形。分尾鳥紋是西周時期最有代表性的紋飾之一，最早出現於西周早期。1972年甘肅靈臺白草坡2號墓出土西周康王時期的兩件隥伯卣上即飾分尾鳥紋[1]，然紋飾簡單稀疏。1978年扶風齊家19號墓出土西周穆、恭時期的鼎、簋、盤、盉等，均飾這種比較精美的分尾鳥紋[2]。1981年陝西長安花園村17號墓出土西周中期的歸夨進觶（M17:38）[3]與這件鳥紋觶形制十分相似，腹部傾垂明顯，是這一時期具有代表性的特點之一。但是歸夨進觶頸下的紋飾爲長尾鳥紋。由此可見，這件鳥紋觶的時代應屬於西周中期。

***Zhi* (wine vessel) with birds**

Mid Western Zhou (late 11th century – late 10th century BC)

Height 12.2cm, length of mouth 10.6cm, width of mouth 7.8cm, depth 10cm, diameter of belly 10.9cm, weight 459.2g

This low-footed vessel, with an oval section, has a trumpet mouth, a contracted neck and a flared bottom. Its mouth rim is rectangular with rounded-off corner. It is decorated with birds, with bifurcated tails around the neck with *leiwen* pattern as the background. The bird is sharp-beaked with ribbon-like feather on the head and two wings bending upwards. The feather on the tail is bifurcated; one is stretching backwards, while the tip of the other is scrolling downwards and the back upwards, which presents a shape of a horizontal S. The design of bifurcate-tailed bird, first appeared in early Western Zhou, is one of the most representative patterns during Western Zhou. Two *you* made for 隥 Bo of King Kang's reign, Western Zhou, which were found in the burial M2 at Baicaopo, Lingtai, Gansu Province in 1972, are decorated with such bifurcate-tailed birds (Gansu 1977:pl.9.1); however, the pattern is simpler and more scattered. Those vessels, such as *ding*, *gui*, *pan* and *he* of King Mu and King Gong's periods in Western Zhou, unearthed from the burial M19 at Qijia, Fufeng County in 1978, are all cast with this kind of elegant bird design (Shaanxi 1979:pl.1.1). A *zhi* made for 歸夨 Jin (M17:38) of mid Western Zhou, from the burial M17 at Huayuancun, Chang'an in Shaanxi Province in 1981, has quite similar shape as this one here, but its belly is more drooping, representing a feature of the period (Shaanxi 1986:pl.1.5). The neck of the 歸夨 Jin *zhi* is decorated with long-tailed birds. Thus, this *zhi* with birds should be dated to the mid Western Zhou.

1.甘肅省博物館文物隊《甘肅靈臺白草坡西周墓》，《考古學報》1977年第2期圖版九‧1。

2.陝西周原考古隊《陝西扶風齊家十九號西周墓》，《文物》1979年第11期圖版一‧1。

3.陝西省文物管理委員會《西周鎬京附近部分墓葬發掘簡報》，《文物》1986年第1期圖版一‧5。

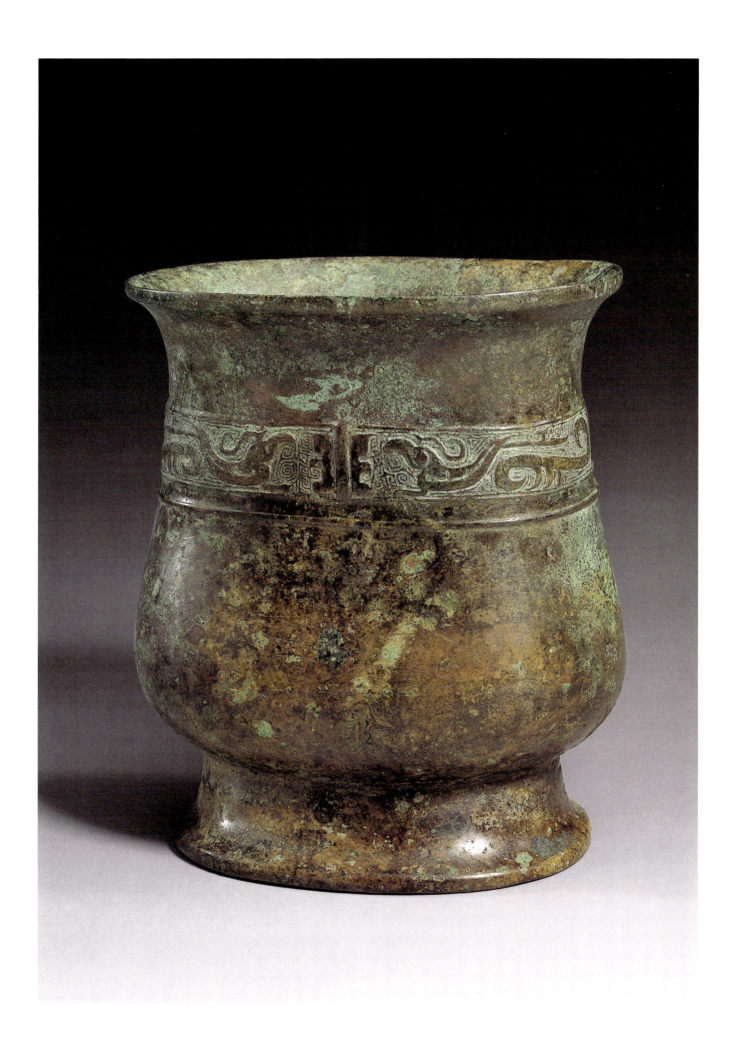

30

晉伯卣

西周中期（公元前11世紀末－前10世紀末）

高27.5厘米　口橫16.2厘米　口縱15.5厘米　腹深15.3厘米　腹徑20.6厘米　重5077.1克

器呈橢圓形，直口高蓋，蓋折沿較高，蓋頂為圈形抓手，蓋面兩側有聳起的犄角，束頸，垂腹，最大徑在腹下部，圈足外撇有折沿，提梁兩端設獸首，獸首為尖喙大耳的貘首形。頸部飾兩道弦紋，前後各有一個高浮雕貘首。蓋和器鑄銘文13字：

晉白（伯）乍（作）氒（厥）酋

宗寶彝其

邁（萬）年永用。

晉伯卣的形制、紋飾與昭王時期的召卣[1]、作冊睘卣很相似[2]，但腹部傾垂又更明顯，年代當晚於此二器。銅卣蓋面兩側出犄角的新形制出現在西周早期偏晚階段，周人銅器的風格開始確立。

***You* (wine vessel) made for Jinbo**

Mid Western Zhou (late 11th century – late 10th century BC)
Height 27.5cm, length of mouth 16.2cm, width of mouth 15.5cm, depth 15.3cm, diameter of belly 20.6cm, weight 5077.1g

This vessel with an oval section has a straight mouth covered by a tall lid, a contracted neck, a depressed body and a splayed foot-ring with a straight rim. The lid has a circular knob and two horn-like projections. Both ends of the handle are decorated with the head of a tapir with a sharp beak and big ears, which also appears on the neck with two bow strings. The lid and the body are cast with a thirteen-character inscription indicating that this vessel was made for Jinbo and would be passed down from generations to generations.

The shape and the decorations of this *you* are very similar to them of the *you* made for Zhao (Chen Peifen 2004:vol.3, p.164) and the *Zuo Ce Qiong you* of King Zhao's reign (Wang Shimin 1999:p.126); however, it is much more drooping than the other two and should belong to a later date. Lids with projecting horns appeared in the early Western Zhou period, representing a time when a characteristic style of Zhou bronzes began to establish.

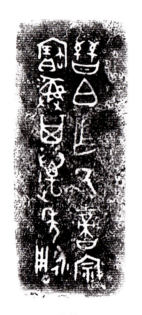

器銘

蓋銘

1.陳佩芬《夏商周青銅器研究》（西周篇·上）第164頁，上海古籍出版社2004年版。

2.王世民等《西周青銅器分期斷代研究》第126頁，文物出版社1999年版。

31

♦乛鼎　西周中期（公元前11世紀末－前10世紀末）
高22.3厘米　口徑20.5厘米　腹深11.1厘米　腹徑20.4厘米　重2224.5克

斂口方脣，立耳稍外傾，腹壁向下逐漸外馳成垂腹狀，最大徑接近腹底，底部略圓，三個細柱足，足內側較平，略向內收。腹部飾花冠式顧龍紋，龍紋呈橫S形，下面有一道凸弦紋，器外底有三角形範綫，外壁和底部煙炱較厚。腹內壁鑄銘文2字：

♦乛。

♦乛鼎的形制、紋飾與恭王時期的標準器十五年趞曹鼎完全相同[1]，這件器物的時代也應屬於西周中期。傳世的還有兩件西周早期的♦乛簋，一件爲上海博物館所藏[2]，一件爲瑞士蘇黎世私人收藏[3]。♦乛鼎與♦乛簋銘文中的“乛”、“乚”應爲反書，二者是同一族徽。

Ding (food vessel) with inscription '♦乛'

Mid Western Zhou (late 11th century – late 10th century BC)
Height 22.3cm, diameter of mouth 20.5cm, depth 11.1cm, diameter of belly 20.4cm, weight 2224.5g

This vessel has a contracted mouth, a flat rim, two upright handles and three slender feet. The body is decorated with S-shaped dragons above a raised ring in the middle. Joints of the moulds left a triangular mark on the base. Much soot residues are found on the exterior and the base. A two-character inscription, '♦乛', is cast on the interior.

Identical in shape and decoration to the _ding_ with the inscription of _shi wu nian que cao_ dated to the fifteenth year of King Gong's reign, this present _ding_ should also belong to the mid Western Zhou period (Chen Peifen 2004:vol.3, p.231). Two ♦乛 _gui_ of the early Western Zhou period are known, one in the Shanghai Museum (Zhongguo 2007:vol.5, fig.3650), and the other in a private collection in Zurich, Switzerland (Zhongguo 2007:vol.5, fig.3649). The 乛 and 乚 appear in reverse in the inscriptions of the ♦乛 _ding_ and ♦乛 _gui_, nonetheless, they are the emblem for the same clan.

1.陳佩芬《夏商周青銅器研究》（西周篇·上）第231頁，上海古籍出版社2004年版。
2.中國社會科學院考古研究所《殷周金文集成》（第五冊）修補增訂本3650，中華書局2007年版。
3.同上3649。

32

仲枏父鬲

西周中期（公元前11世紀末－前10世紀末）

高14厘米　口徑19.4厘米　腹深8.6厘米　腹徑17.4厘米　重1888克

寬沿，短頸，鼓腹下承三個蹄形足，蹄足內側內凹，足底粗大。腹部飾粗獷的象鼻龍紋，器身有扉棱，口沿至腹部鑄有銘文七行39字：

佳（唯）六月初吉

師湯父有嗣（司）

中（仲）枏父乍（作）寶

鬲用敢卿（饗）孝于

皇且（祖）丂（考）用旛（祈）

眉壽其萬年

子子孫孫其永寶用。

仲枏父鬲的形制和紋飾風格是西周中期以後的典型樣式。陝西永壽好畤河陸續出土了幾批仲枏父[1]。目前存世的仲枏父器組共有九鬲、二簋、一匕，除這件鬲外的其他八件分別藏於西安市文物管理委員會、武功縣文化館、陝西歷史博物館、上海博物館。《考古圖》曾著錄了一件仲枏父甗[2]，原定名為仲信父方旅甗，傳為乾州好畤出土，今此器已不知下落。

仲枏父鬲銘文中提到的師湯父與仲枏父是同時代的人物。傳世的師湯父鼎，學者多據其銘文定為恭王時器。1991年陝西扶風縣法門鎮齊家村1號墓亦出土了一件師湯父鼎（91M1：2506）[3]，根據器形和紋飾斷定亦為西周中期的器物。

Li (cooking vessel) made for Zhongnanfu

Mid Western Zhou (late 11th century – late 10th century BC)
Height 14cm, diameter of mouth 19.4cm, depth 8.6cm, diameter of belly 17.4cm, weight 1888g

This *li* has a wide and flat rim, a short neck, and a bulging belly with three hoof-shaped feet. Dragons with the nose of an elephant decorate the belly with flanges. A thirty-nine-character inscription in seven columns is cast running from the rim down the interior, indicating that this vessel is made for Zhongnanfu and should be passed down from generations to generations.

This *li*'s form and decorative patterns are typical of mid Western Zhou. Bronzes made for Zhongnanfu have been excavated at different times from Haochouhe of Yongshou in Shaanxi Province (Shaanxi 1964:pp.20-25; Wu Zhenfeng 1979:pp.119-121). By now, Zhongnanfu vessels in existence include nine *li*, two *gui* and one *bi* (spoon). Apart from this present example, the other eight *li* are known in the collections of the Municipal Administration of Cultural Relics of Xi'an, the Cultural Center of Wugong County, the History Museum of Shaanxi Province and the Shanghai

---

1.陝西省文物管理委員會《陝西省永壽縣、武功縣出土西周銅器》，《文物》1964年7期第20-25頁；吳鎮烽等《陝西永壽、藍田出土西周青銅器》，《考古》1979年第2期第119-121頁。

2.《考古圖》2·21。

3.羅西章《陝西周原新出土的青銅器》，《考古》1999年第4期圖版三·4。

Museum. A *yan* steamer made for Zhongnanfu was published in *Kaogu Tu* of the Song period (Kaogu Tu, 2.21). Originally known as Zhongxinfu Fanglü *yan*, the vessel was said to be found in Haochou, Qian Prefecture, but its present whereabouts is unknown.

Shitangfu, mentioned in the inscription of this piece, and Zhongnanfu should be contemporaries. Scholars generally agree that an extant *ding* made for Shitangfu should be dated according to its inscription to the period of King Gong's reign. In 1991 another *ding* made for Shitangfu (91M1:2506) was unearthed from a burial (M1) at Qijiacun, Famenzhen in Fufeng, Shaanxi Province (Luo Xizhang 1999:pl.3.4), and it is dated to the mid Western Zhou, judging from its shape and decoration.

33

智 簋　西周中期（公元前11世紀末－前10世紀末）
高11.8厘米　口徑21.4厘米　腹深9.4厘米　腹徑20.9厘米　重2546.3克

　　侈口，腹部下垂，整器顯得矮胖，高圈足外撇有折沿，獸首形附耳下有小鈎狀垂珥。頸部飾回首龍紋，長體卷尾，呈橫S形，長冠下垂後上卷，其下飾一道弦紋，頸部中間飾突起的小獸首，圈足飾兩道弦紋。腹內底鑄銘文六行50字：

　　唯四月初吉丙午王

　　令（命）智易（賜）截（緇）市（韍）同黃（衡）□□

　　曰用吏（事）嗣（司）奠（鄭）駱馬弔（叔）

　　朕（朕）父加（嘉）智曆用赤金

　　一勺（鈞）用對揚王休乍（作）寶

　　簋子子孫孫其永寶。

　　智簋的形制、紋飾與西周中期的靜簋[1]很相似，口沿下都飾長冠迤邐上卷的顧龍紋。靜簋腹部飾垂冠顧首的大鳥紋，但是智簋腹部不施紋飾。這件器物的資料曾經發表[2]。以“智”爲名的人物在金文中所見有十二器，諸器的年代由西周穆王、恭王延伸至厲王時期，金文中所稱之“智”并非同一人。

***Gui* (food vessel) made for Hu**

Mid Western Zhou (late 11th century – late 10th century BC)
Height 11.8cm, diameter of mouth 21.4cm, depth 9.4cm, diameter of belly 20.9cm, weight 2546.3g

This high-footed *gui* looks short and stout with a slightly flared mouth, a drooping belly and two looped handles with animal head. Below each handle, there is a lug in the shape of

a small hook. Small animal heads in relief appear in the middle of the neck, which is decorated with a continuous band of S-shaped dragons. Below the dragons is a raised band and two more raised bands on the foot. In the interior there is a fifty-character inscription in six columns at the bottom, indicating that the *gui* was made for Hu.

The shape and decoration of this *gui* are similar to a *gui* with the inscription '*jing*' of the mid Western Zhou period (Wang Shimin 1999:p.61), in particular, the dragons below the rim. The Jing *gui* has in addition birds on the lower body.

Published bronzes and their inscriptions with the name Hu are known (Cheung Kwong Yue 2000:pp.86-89). There are at least twelve related vessels with dates spanning a rather long period from Kings Mu, Gong to Li, all of the Western Zhou. This indicates that 'Hu' could not have been referred to the same person.

1.王世民等《西周青銅器分期斷代研究》第61頁，文物出版社1999年版。
2.張光裕《新見智簋銘文對金文研究的意義》，《文物》2000年6期第86-89頁。

34

芮 伯 簋

西周中期（公元前11世紀末－前10世紀末）

高28.7厘米　口徑19.1厘米　腹深11.7厘米　腹徑19.5厘米　重4722.5克

侈口，有蓋，垂腹，最大徑接近腹底，圈足稍外侈，圈足與方座連接，獸首形附耳下有長方形垂珥，蓋頂爲圈形捉手，捉手有三穿。蓋頂、頸部、腹部、方座上均飾雲雷紋襯底的分尾鳳鳥紋，鳳頭顧盼，長喙內彎，鳳冠下垂上卷，雙翅上揚，尾羽分爲兩段，上端上卷，下端下卷，圈足飾斜角雲目紋，方座臺面飾獸面紋，器蓋同銘兩行8字：

芮白（伯）乍（作）旝（旂）

公日寶簋。

1980年山東黃縣莊頭村1號墓出土的兩件芮公叔簋[1]與此件的形制、紋飾完全一致。芮公叔簋銘曰："芮公叔乍（作）旝（旂）宮寶簋。"1961年陝西長安張家坡窖藏所出穆王時期的盂簋[2]與芮伯簋的形制和紋飾也很相似。因此，這件器物的時代定爲西周中期是合適的。

Gui (food vessel) made for Ruibo

Mid Western Zhou (late 11th century – late 10th century BC)
Height 28.7cm, diameter of mouth 19.1cm, depth 11.7cm, diameter of belly 19.5cm, weight 4722.5g

This lidded vessel has a slightly flared mouth, a drooping belly, two looped handles with animal heads and a slightly splayed foot-ring connected to a square pedestal base. A rectangular lug hangs from each handle. The lid has a circular knob with three apertures. Pheonixes with long beaks, bifurcated tails and stretched wings on a *leiwen* ground appear on the lid, neck, belly and pedestal base. The foot-ring is decorated with a pattern of angular cloud eyes and the top of the square pedestal base animal masks. An inscription indicating this *gui* is made for Ruibo is cast on the interior.

The shape and decoration of two *gui* made for Ruigongshu, unearthed from a burial (M1) at Zhuangtoucun, Huangxian, Shandong Province in 1980, are identical with this *gui* here (Wang Xiping & Tang Luting 1986:p.71, fig.9). A *gui* with the inscription '*meng*' of the King Mu's reign was unearthed from Zhangjiapo of Chang'an in Shaanxi Province in 1961, and its shape and decoration are quite similar to the Ruigongshu *gui* (Zhongguo 1965:pl.3). Therefore, it is reasonable to date this *gui* to the mid Western Zhou period.

1. 王錫平、唐禄庭《山東黃縣莊頭西周墓清理簡報》，《文物》1986年第8期第71頁圖九。
2. 中國科學院考古研究所《長安張家坡西周銅器群》圖版三，文物出版社1965年版。

蓋銘　　　　　　　　　　　　　　　　器銘

35

龍紋盤 西周中期（公元前11世紀末－前10世紀末）
高11.8厘米　口徑38.2厘米　腹深8.4厘米　腹徑33.7厘米　重5350克

口沿外折，腹壁圓轉內收，腹部兩側有附耳，附耳上端高出口沿，圈足外撇形成高階。腹部飾雲雷紋襯底的顧龍紋，龍體呈橫S形，體形修長，尾巴上卷，龍冠與龍頭脫離內卷。

這件龍紋盤的形制與1954年陝西長安普渡村所出的長由盤[1]和1976年陝西扶風莊白1號窖藏所出的史墻盤[2]相同。從附耳聳出口沿的程度來看，更近於長由盤。長由盤與同墓所出的長由盉同爲穆王時器，史墻盤則爲恭王時代的標準器。因此，這件龍紋盤的時代應在西周中期早段。

盤內有銘文一篇。

Pan (water vessel) with dragons

Mid Western Zhou (late 11th century – late 10th century BC)
Height 11.8cm, diameter of mouth 38.2cm, depth 8.4cm, diameter of belly 33.7cm, weight 5350g

Two handles extend from the sides of the belly and rise beyond the everted rim. The footring is splayed with a straight rim. The belly is decorated with S-shaped dragons on a _leiwen_ ground. The dragon has a slender body and an upward scrolled tail. In the interior, an apocryphal inscription is found at the bottom.

Its shape is the same as a _pan_ with the inscription '_chang fu_' excavated from Puducun, Chang'an County in Shaanxi Province in 1954 (Shaanxi 1957:pl.5.6), and another _pan_ with the inscription '_shi qiang_' found in a hoard at Zhuangbai, Fufeng County, Shaanxi Province in 1976 (Shaanxi 1978:pl.5.1). The Chang Fu _pan_ provides a comparable example with respect to the handles exceeding the rim. The Chang Fu pan and and the Chang Fu _he_ from the same burial belong to King Mu's period, while the Shi Qiang _pan_ is a standard specimen of the King Gong bronzes. Thus, this vessel here should be dated to the beginning of the mid Western Zhou period.

1.陝西省文管會《長安普渡村西周墓的發掘》，《考古學報》1957年第1期圖版伍‧6。
2.陝西周原考古隊《陝西扶風莊白一號西周青銅器窖藏發掘簡報》，《文物》1978年第3期圖版伍‧1。

36

伯[⚔]父簋

西周中期（公元前11世紀末－前10世紀末）
高17.1厘米　口徑20厘米　腹深12.1厘米　腹徑24.6厘米　重5220克

敞口，失蓋，鼓腹，腹部兩側有獸首形環耳，下有長方形垂珥，圈足下設三小獸形足，足端粗厚外折。頸部飾變形獸面紋，腹部飾瓦楞紋，圈足飾斜角雲目紋。器內底鑄銘文七行67字：

佳（唯）王九月初吉庚午王

出自成周南征伐及（服）寬（子）

廣桐滴伯[⚔]父從王伐

窺（親）執訊十父馘廿得俘

金五十匀（鈞）用作寶簋對揚

用亯（享）于文祖考用易（賜）眉亯（享）

壽其萬年子子孫孫永寶用。

這件伯[⚔]父簋的形制和主體紋飾與1963年陝西藍田輞川出土的弭伯簋[1]和1961年陝西長安張家坡窖藏出土的元年師旋簋[2]完全相同。根據銘文弭伯簋的年代可推定爲恭王前後，元年師旋簋當爲夷王前後。其圈足所飾的斜角雲目紋，又與故宮博物院所藏的諫簋[3]相同，年代應在孝王前後。因此，這件簋應屬孝、夷時期的器物。李學勤先生曾著文討論過另外兩件同銘伯[⚔]父簋的銘文[4]。

***Gui* (food vessel) made for Bo [⚔] fu**

Mid Western Zhou (late 11th century – late 10th century BC)
Height 17.1cm, diameter of mouth 20cm, depth 12.1cm, diameter of belly 24.6cm, weight 5220g

This vessel has a contracted mouth, a convex belly and two looped handles with animal heads. Below each handle, there is a rectangular pendant projection. The original is missing. The foot-ring stands on three small animal-headed feet, the tips of which are short, bulging and everted. The neck is decorated with stylized animal masks; the belly with relief bands; the foot-ring with angular cloud-eye pattern. The interior bottom is cast with an inscription of sixty-seven characters in seven columns, indicating the vessel was made for Bo [⚔] fu.

1. 應新、子敬《記陝西藍田縣出土的西周銅簋》，《文物》1966年第1期第5頁圖一。
2. 中國科學院考古研究所《長安張家坡西周銅器群》圖版柒，文物出版社1965年版。
3. 故宮博物院編《故宮青銅器》第203頁，紫禁城出版社1999年版。
4. 李學勤《談西周屬王時器伯[⚔]父簋》，《安作璋先生史學研究六十周年紀念文集》第86－89頁，齊魯書社2007年版。

The decoration and shape of this *gui* are exactly the same as the *gui* made for Mibo, which was excavated from Wangchuan, Lantian County, Shaanxi Province in 1963 and is roughly dated to King Gong's period of Western Zhou according to its inscription (Ying Xin & Zi Jing 1966:p.5, fig.1). It is also identical to the Shi 旋 *gui* of the first year of the King Yi's period, unearthed from Zhangjiapo, Chang'an, Shaanxi Province in 1961 (Zhongguo 1965:pl.7). The angular cloud eye pattern on the foot-ring, however, is the same as that on the *gui* inscribed *jian*, in the collection of the Palace Museum, Beijing, which is dated to around King Xiao's reign (Gugong 1999:p.203). So this vessel should be cast in the period between the reigns of King Xiao and King Yi of Western Zhou. Prof. Li Xueqin has made a research on another two *gui* with the same inscription (Li Xueqin 2007:pp.86-89).

37

變形龍紋爵 西周晚期（公元前9世紀上半葉－前771年）

高6.3厘米　口橫7.5厘米　口縱6.6厘米　腹深4厘米　腹徑最大8.2厘米　重348克

　　勺口微斂，鼓腹，圈足外侈有折沿，曲柄從腹部伸出，另一側有獸首形鋬。柄部飾鏤空雙首龍紋，上腹部飾變形龍紋，下腹部飾瓦楞紋，圈足飾鏤空垂鱗紋。

　　這種形制的爵與宋代以來所定名的爵大不相同，有的稱爲"斗"，有的稱爲"勺"，日本學者林巳奈夫先生稱之爲"瓚"。1976年陝西扶風莊白2號窖藏出土西周晚期伯公父爵的形制與此十分相似[1]，銘文中自銘爲"金爵"，但伯公父爵上缺少了一個獸首形鋬。2006年陝西扶風五郡窖藏出土的三件爵的形制與此件幾乎完全相同[2]，唯獨口沿下的紋飾稍有差異。故宮博物院收藏一件鳥鋬爵[3]，形制十分獨特，饒有趣味。《說文》云："器象爵者，取其雀鳴之意。"這件鳥鋬爵的形制不意與《說文》暗合，然仍爲孤證。《三禮圖》載有匏爵，係刻木製成，形制亦爲近似。李零先生認爲這種形制的器物應相當於禮書中的"廢爵"。[4]

　　扶風五郡窖藏的時代早晚有別，出土時三件爵置於白湄父簋內，而白湄父簋依其形制斷定應爲西周晚期。這件變形龍紋爵放在西周晚期似乎妥當。

　　這種爵是在傳統飲酒器觚、觶逐漸消亡的背景下出現的。從形制來看，此爵前有獸首形鋬，後有曲柄，用以挹酒實爲不便。伯公父爵銘文自稱"用獻、用酌、用孝"，其功能正是作爲獻酌之用。

1.陝西周原考古隊《陝西雲塘、莊白二號西周銅器窖藏》，《文物》1978年11期圖版三·1。

2.寶雞市考古研究所、扶風縣博物館《陝西扶風五郡西村西周青銅器窖藏發掘簡報》，《文物》2007年第8期第11頁圖16。

3.故宮博物院編《故宮青銅器》第285頁，紫禁城出版社1999年版。

4.李零《鑠古鑄今——考古發現和復古藝術》第47-49頁，香港中文大學出版社2005年版。

Jue (wine vessel) with stylized dragons

Late Western Zhou (first half of the 9th century – 771 BC)
Height 6.3cm, length of mouth 7.5cm, width of mouth 6.6cm, depth 4cm, diameter of belly 8.2cm, weight 348g

This *jue* has a slightly contracted mouth, a round body and a splayed foot-ring with a straight rim. Its horizontal handle is decorated two-headed dragons in openwork, and in the opposite side is an animal head loop-handle. The upper part of the body has stylized dragons, and the lower part has corrugated design. The foot-ring has pendant scales in openwork.

Sometimes known as *dou* or *shao* (ladle), or *zan* called by Minao Hayashi, the present *jue* is different from a later type of *jue* known since the Song dynasty. It is similar in shape to a piece of the late Western Zhou period from a hoard (No.2) at Zhuangbai, Fufeng County, Shaanxi Province in 1976, which is labeled '*jin* (bronze) *jue*' in the inscription and was made for Bogongfu yet it does not have an animal-head loop-handle (Shaanxi 1978b:pl.3.1). Three *jue* unearthed from a hoard at Wujun, Fufeng County, Shaanxi Province in 2006 are in the same shape, with the sole difference in the decoration below the rim (Baoji 2007:p.11, fig.16). In the Palace Museum, Beijing is a unique *jue* with a bird-shaped loop-handle. According to *Shuowen Jiezi* by Xu Shen of the Eastern Han, the reason for this kind of vessel being called *jue* was based on a connection between a *que* (sparrow) and *jue* (Gugong 1999:p285). The *jue* in the Palace Museum bears, however, a single evidence. In *Sanli Tu* (The Three Rituals) compiled by Nie Chongyi of the Song period, there is a Pao *jue* made of wood, which has a shape similar to the unique *jue* in Beijing. Prof. Li Ling suggests that the type of vessel should refer to '*fei jue*' in ancient documents on rituals (Li Ling 2005:pp.47-49).

The objects found at Wujun, Fufeng County are dated to different times. The three *jue* mentioned above were found inside a *gui* made for Baimeifu and this *gui* is dated to late Western Zhou. It seems reasonable to date this *jue* with stylized dragons to the late Western Zhou period likewise.

This type of *jue* appeared when the popularity of *zhi* and *gu*, the traditional wine-drinking vessels, waned. In fact, it is not practical to spoon wine with such a *jue* having a handle and a loop-handle. The inscription of the Bogongfu *jue* indicates that it is used to pour wine and offer a toast to the honored guests.

38

晉侯穌鼎

西周晚期（公元前9世紀上半葉－前771年）

高23.4厘米　口徑26.9厘米　腹深13.6厘米　腹徑25.6厘米　重4580.8克

　　折沿，腹部爲半球狀，下收爲圜底，腹部兩側有附耳，並有小銅棍與口沿相接，三蹄形足不明顯，足根粗大，足內側較平。腹部飾重環紋和一道弦紋。腹內壁鑄銘文三行13字：

　　晉侯穌乍（作）

　　寶尊鼎其

　　萬年永寶用。

　　晉侯穌鼎共有五件，形制、紋飾、銘文均相同，唯大小依次遞減。[1]1992年山西天馬曲村遺址北趙晉侯墓地8號墓出土，其他四件分藏於上海博物館、曲沃縣博物館和山西省考古研究所[2]。銘文中的晉侯穌與同墓所出的晉侯穌編鐘的器主爲同一個人，晉侯穌編鐘根據銘文定爲西周厲王時期。據《史記·晉世家》索隱引《世本》所記，晉獻侯名穌（蘇）。這是晉侯墓地中所出晉侯諸器的銘文中唯一能與史書記載相對應的人物。

Ding (food vessel) made for Marquis Su of Jin

Late Western Zhou (first half of the 9th century – 771 BC)
Height 23.4cm, diameter of mouth 26.9cm, depth 13.6cm, diameter of belly 25.6cm, weight 4580.8g

This vessel has an everted rim. The handles on the sides of the body are joined to the rim by small horizontal projections. The body, supported by three hoof-shaped feet, is decorated with segmented rings and scales in addition to a raised band. On the interior is a thirteen-character inscription indicating that this _ding_ is made for Marquis Su of Jin.

Five _ding_ made for Marquis Su of Jin in varied size are known. They are identical in shape, decoration and inscription (Zhou Ya 2002:pp.446-451). They were unearthed from a burial (No.8) in Tianma, Shanxi Province in 1992. Besides this one, the other four are now in the collections of the Shanghai Museum, the Quwo County Museum and the Shanxi Provincial Institute of Cultural Relics and Archaeology respectively (Shanghai 2002:pp.101-103). A set of chime bells made for Marquis Su of Jin, the person mentioned in the inscription of this _ding_, was unearthed from the same burial. The chime bells are dated to King Li's reign of the Western Zhou period, As recorded in _Shiji_ (Records of the Grand Historian) by Sima Qian, the name of Marquis Xian of Jin is Su, who is the only identified person recorded in historical texts appearing in the inscriptions on vessels made for Marquis of the Jin State.

1.周亞《關於晉侯穌鼎件數的探討》，《晋侯墓地出土青銅器國際學術研討會論文集》第446-451頁，上海書畫出版社2002年版。
2.上海博物館《晉國奇珍——山西晉侯墓群出土文物精品》第101-103頁，上海人民美術出版社2002年版。

39

雁侯簋

西周晚期（公元前9世紀上半葉－前771年）

高23.1厘米　口徑19.2厘米　腹深11.9厘米　腹徑24.5厘米　重4589.4克

　　斂口，高蓋折沿，蓋頂有圈形捉手，蓋緣有兩道弦紋，鼓腹，腹部兩側有獸首形環耳，下有長方形垂珥，圈足下設三小獸首形足，足端粗厚外折。蓋頂、頸部、圈足飾鱗紋，蓋沿飾兩道弦紋，腹部飾瓦楞紋，蓋內鑄銘文九行82字。器內底鑄銘文三行14字：

雁（應）侯乍（作）姬邍（原）

母尊簋其邁（萬）

年永寶用。

　　這件雁侯簋的形制、紋飾與西周晚期的元年師兌簋、三年師兌簋完全相同[1]。宋人著錄中有一件雁侯簋[2]，銘文僅有摹本，形制、紋飾也與此件相同。按照尺寸換算，著錄的雁侯簋通高19厘米、口徑18.7厘米、腹深12.7厘米、腹徑24厘米，重4431克。除通高外，其餘數值十分接近。但從所摹器物的形制可以看出，簋的三足可能殘缺。因此，這件雁侯簋與宋人著錄的雁侯簋當爲同銘器。但是此器的蓋銘與器銘不配，若蓋銘無誤，應該是在隨葬中擺放錯了。

Gui (food vessel) made for Marquis of Ying

Late Western Zhou (first half of the 9th century – 771 BC)

Height 23.1cm, diameter of mouth 19.2cm, depth 11.9cm, diameter of belly 24.5cm, weight 4589.4g

This *gui* is composed of a contracted mouth, a cover with a fitted lid, a convex belly and two looped handles with animal heads. Below each handle, there is a rectangular pendant. The foot-ring stands on three small animal-headed feet, the tips of which are short, bulging and everted. The top of the lid, the neck and the ring–foot are decorated with segmented scales. Along the rim of lid is carved with two bow strings; relief bands wrap round the belly. A fourteen-character inscription is cast inside the vessel, indicating this *gui* was made for Marquis of the Ying State, while the lid has a different inscription of eighty-two characters and arranged in nine columns. .

This *gui* is identical in shape and decoration to two Shi Dui *gui* of the late Western Zhou (Chen Peifen 2004:vol.3, p.290 and p.294). A *gui* made for Marquis of Ying, with the same shape and decoration, was published in Song catalogues (*Kaogu Tu*, 3.17; *Xuanhe Bogu Tu*, 17.10; *Lidai Zhongding Yiqi Kuanshi Fatie*, 122; *Xiaotang Jigulu*, 60). Its dimensions are: overall height 19cm, diameter of mouth 18.7cm, depth 12.7cm, diameter of belly 24cm, and weight 4431g. The measurements are very close to the present piece except for the height. Judging from the illustrations in the catalogues, the three feet of that *gui* were mostly likely damaged. This would explain the difference in height. It is obvious that this present *gui* has a similar body shape and identical inscription to the one published in the Song catalogues. The unmatched inscription on the lid, however, poses a problem. One possibility is that the inscription was done later; another possibility is that the lid, from a different vessel, was misplaced on this bowl in the burial.

1.陳佩芬《夏商周青銅器研究》（西周篇·上）第290、294頁，上海古籍出版社2004年版。

2.《考古圖》3·17，《宣和博古圖》17·10，《歷代鐘鼎彝器款識法帖》122，《嘯堂集古錄》60。

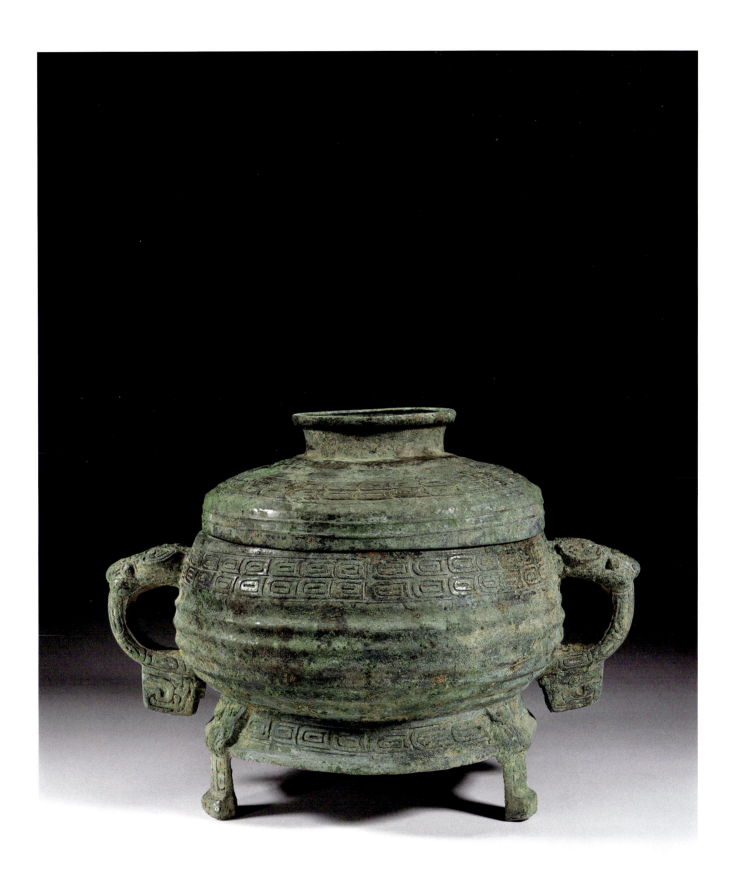

113

器銘

蓋銘

40

晉侯鮒盨　西周晚期（公元前9世紀上半葉－前771年）

高17.4厘米　口橫21.5厘米　口縱13.7厘米　腹深7.4厘米　重3085.5克

　　器呈圓角長方形，蓋作長方形盝頂式，蓋沿方折，蓋頂亦有四個環形丫狀鈕，可却置。腹壁較直，獸首形附耳下有垂珥，矮圈足下接四個環形丫狀小足，蓋面和器身飾顧龍紋和瓦楞紋，圈足飾鱗紋，蓋和器内有銘文六行30字：

　　佳（唯）正月初吉

　　庚寅晉侯鮒

　　作寶尊彶（及）盨

　　其用田獸（狩）甚（湛）

　　樂于邍（原）𤔲（隰）其

　　邁（萬）年永寶用。

　　銅盨是西周中期出現的新器物，盛行於西周晚期，春秋早期以後絕迹。盨是由簋演變而來的，二者有很深的淵源，它的產生是周人重食文化的表現。這件晉侯鮒盨的形制十分奇巧，不同於一般形制的盨。

　　晉侯鮒盨共有兩組六器，1992年山西曲沃縣北趙村晉侯墓地出土，曾流散於香港，逐漸回收。這一組共有四件，形制、紋飾、銘文均相同，其餘三件現藏上海博物館[1]。

Xu (food vessel) made for Marquis Dui of Jin

Late Western Zhou (first half of the 9th century – 771 BC)
Height 17.4cm, length of mouth 21.5cm, width of mouth 13.7cm, depth 7.4cm, weight 3085.5g

The round-cornered, rectangular *xu* has a box-shaped lid with four loop knobs topped by Y-shaped finials which can serve as feet when the cover is removed and placed upside down. Its two handles in the form of animal heads have pendent lugs. The low foot-ring is supported by four loop feet like the knobs of the lid. The lid and the body are decorated with dragons and tiles. Around the foot-ring is a band of double oblongs. A thirty-character inscription is cast in the interiors of both the cover and the body, which indicates that the *xu* was made for Marquis Dui of Jin in the first month, and could be used during the period of hunting.

Xu appeared in the mid Western Zhou period and was commonly used in the late Western Zhou, but disappeared after the early Spring and Autumn period. It evolved from the *gui*, and its birth is a symbol of the food culture of the Zhou people.

Two sets of *xu* made for Marquis Dui of Jin, consisting of six pieces, were unearthed from the burials of the Marquises of Jin at Beizhaocun, Quwo County, Shanxi Province in 1992. Some of them smuggled and dispersed in Hong Kong, have returned to the mainland. The current *xu*, as one of the four extant pieces in a set, is in the Shouyang Studio Collection, while the other three are in the Shanghai Museum Collection (Chen Peifen 2004 :vol. 4, pp.499-501).

1.陳佩芬《夏商周青銅器研究》（西周篇・下）第499–501頁，上海古籍出版社2004年版。

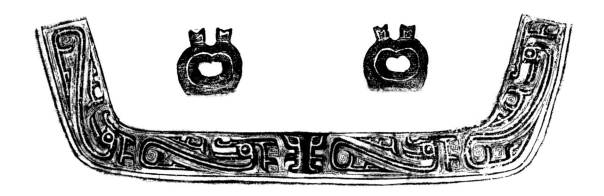

器銘

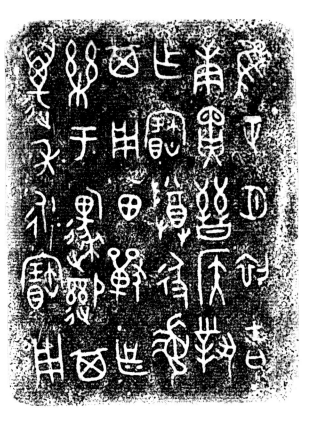

蓋銘

41

柞鐘

西周晚期（公元前9世紀上半葉–前771年）

高43.2厘米　舞橫21.1厘米　舞縱18.4厘米　鼓橫25.8厘米　鼓縱18.8厘米　重16150克

　　此鐘爲甬鐘，鐘體呈合瓦形，甬和腔體相通，但殘留有範土，甬上設旋、幹，于之弧曲較小。旋飾獸目紋，舞部飾雲紋，篆間飾兩頭龍紋，正鼓部飾對稱的顧首龍紋，右側鼓飾一顧首龍紋。鐘體內壁有凹槽八條，其中正面和背面的正鼓部、左側鼓、右側鼓部、左銑、右銑各一。學者們的研究表明，西周時期的甬鐘分爲四個型別，這類形制的鐘屬於Ⅳ型中的3式，Ⅳ型鐘數量最多，其時代均爲西周中晚期[1]。

　　鉦部及左鼓部鑄銘六行：

史柞乍（作）朕皇考龢鐘用㽙

□朕皇考用□□無疆康虩

屯（純）魯永命用祈多福柞其

眉壽萬

年子子孫孫永

寶用享。

　　據銘文，這件鐘爲一套編鐘之一件，根據尺寸和測音結果推斷[2]，可能是編鐘中的第三件。"柞"亦見於1960年陝西省扶風縣齊家村窖藏出土的柞鐘銘文[3]。

**_Zhong_ (bell) made
for Zuo**

Late Western Zhou (first half of the 9th century – 771 BC)
Height 43.2cm, length of top 21.1cm, width of top 18.4cm, length of bottom 25.8cm, width of bottom 18.8cm, weight 16150g

The _zhong_, taking the form of two joined roof tiles, has a cylindrical handle with a burl and a loop lug, and a lip in a small arc. Inside the hollow handle are remains of clay cores which join to the interior of the bell. The burl is decorated with animal eyes, and the flat top with clouds. Between the rows of bosses are dragons with two heads. Outside the central point of the lip are two symmetrical dragons looking backward, and on the right corner is also a dragon. Eight flutes can be seen in the interior of the bell.

The bells with a long cylindrical handle, known as _yong zhong_, of the Western Zhou period can be divided into four types. The current bell belongs to the 3rd group of the 4th type dating from the mid and late Western Zhou (Wang Shimin 1999:sec. 11 in ch. 3).

An inscription in six columns is cast on the central section and the left corner of the bell, which indicates that the _zhong_, as one of a set of bell chimes, is made for Zuo who hoped that his father would live a long life with much happiness and that the object would be treasured by his descendants forever. According to its size and musical scale (The examination on musical scale by Shi Yin in the Shanghai Music College shows that the tone of the central point of the lip is a^1 and the tone of the corner is c^2), the _zhong_ should be the No.3 in the set of bell chimes. The character _zuo_ is also seen in the inscription cast on a _zhong_ bell excavated among a hoard of bronzes at Qijiacun, Fufeng County, Shaanxi Province in 1960 (Shaanxi 1980:vol. 2, pls.156-163).

1.參見王世民等《西周青銅器分期斷代研究》第三章第一一節，文物出版社1999年版。

2.經上海音樂學院史寅先生測音，正鼓音爲a^1，側鼓音爲c^2。

3.陝西省考古研究所等《陝西出土商周青銅器（二）》圖版156至163，文物出版社1980年版。

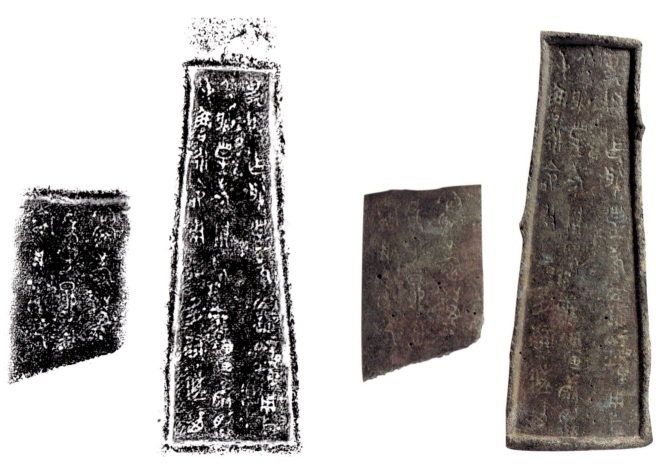

42

速 鐘 西周晚期（公元前9世紀上半葉－前771年）

高27.4厘米　舞橫13.5厘米　舞縱10.8　鼓橫15.3厘米　鼓縱11.4厘米　重5450.5克

此鐘爲甬鐘，封衡，甬上設旋、幹，甬不與體腔相通，兩銑較侈，于之弧曲較大。旋飾獸目交連紋，舞部飾雲紋，篆間飾變形獸紋，正鼓部飾對稱的顧首龍紋，右側鼓飾一鸞鳥紋。鐘體內壁有凹槽七條，其中正面和背面的正鼓部、左側鼓、右側鼓部各一，右銑一。

鉦部及左鼓部鑄銘五行25字（包括重文5）：

追孝邵各喜侃

前文人前文人嚴在上

數數象象

降余多

福康龎。

這是一篇完整銘文中的一段，從銘文的辭意看，當尚有一件鐘的銘文接於此鐘之後。

1985年陝西眉縣馬家鎮楊家村發現一青銅樂器窖藏[1]，其中，乙組編鐘即速鐘共四件，從音樂性能的檢測看，這四件鐘屬於成套編鐘，編次爲Ⅱ號、Ⅰ號、Ⅲ號、Ⅳ號，整套編鐘應爲八件，尚缺第一、五、六、七鐘[2]。Ⅰ、Ⅱ、Ⅲ號鐘銘文一致，皆單獨成爲完整的一篇，而Ⅳ號鐘的鑄銘是整篇銘文的最後部分，所以Ⅳ號鐘也是這套編鐘的最後一件，與測音結果相合。

這件鐘的形制和紋飾與速鐘完全相同，形制資料比Ⅳ號速鐘略大一些，而銘文也排在Ⅳ號速鐘的前面，是爲這套編鐘的最後第二件。從測音結果看，其音樂性能的排序亦完全證實了這個結論[3]。

美國克利夫蘭博物館也收藏一件速鐘，形制與窖藏出土的四件速鐘完全相同，銘文的內容、行款與Ⅰ、Ⅱ、Ⅲ號鐘相同，同屬於一套[4]。

在上述六件速鐘中，克利夫蘭博物館藏鐘和Ⅱ號鐘，右鼓部均無鸞鳥紋，西周中晚期的編鐘，前兩件的右側鼓部是沒有紋飾的，從第三件起才有小鸞鳥等作爲第二基音擊奏點的標誌，因此這兩件速鐘應爲這套編鐘的頭兩件。而從形制資料和音階結構來看，克利夫蘭博物館藏鐘應是這套編鐘的第一件。這樣已發現的六件速鐘的排序依次爲：克利夫蘭博物館藏鐘（1）、Ⅱ號鐘（2）、Ⅰ號鐘（3）、Ⅲ號鐘（4）、本文的鐘（7）、Ⅳ號鐘（8）。

1.劉懷軍《眉縣出土一批窖藏青銅樂器》，《文博》1987年第2期第17頁。

2.方建軍《中國音樂文物大系·陝西卷》第64頁，大象出版社1996年版。

3.經上海音樂學院史寅先生測音，正鼓音爲d³，側鼓音爲#f³。

4.方建軍《美國收藏的速鐘及相關問題》，《天津音樂學院學報》2007年第2期。

Zhong (bell) made for Lai

Late Western Zhou (first half of the 9th century – 771 BC)
Height 27.4cm, length of top 13.5cm, width of top 10.8cm, length of bottom 15.3cm, width of bottom 11.4cm, weight 5450.5g

Also as a *yong zhong*, the bell has a long cylindrical handle with closed ends, a burl, a loop lug and a lip in a wide arc. The burl is decorated with patterns of *shoumu jiaolian* (animals connected by the eyes), and the flat top with clouds. Between the rows of bosses are stylized animals. Outside the central point of the lip are two symmetrical dragons looking backward, and on the right corner is a phoenix. Seven flutes can be seen in the interior of the bell.

An inscription with twenty-five characters in five columns is cast on the central section and the left corner of the bell. After reading the text, we know that this should be the first part of an inscription and the rest of the text is cast on another *zhong*.

A hoard of bronze musical instruments was unearthed from Yangjiacun, Majiazhen, Meixian, Shaanxi Province in 1985 (Liu Huaijun 1987:p.17). Among these objects, there are four *zhong* made for Lai. These bells should be numbered as 2, 3, 4 and 8 in a set of eight bell chimes in accordance with the musical scale (Fang Jianjun 1996:p.64).

The current bell is the same in form and decoration as the Lai *zhong* found in Yangjiacun. It is a little bigger than the No.8 bell and its inscription also precedes that of the latter in the context. So this *zhong* from the Shouyang Studio should be the No.7, which has also been proved by scale examination (The examination on musical scale by Shi Yin in the Shanghai Music College shows that the tone of the central point of the lip is d[3] and the tone of the corner is f[3].).

Another Lai *zhong* in the collection of the Cleveland Museum is identical in form to the four *zhong* unearthed from Shaanxi (Fang Jianjun 2007). Its inscription bears the same content and style as the No.2, 3 and 4 bells. Judging by the size, decoration and musical scale, it should be the No.1 of the set of bell chimes.

43

龍紋鼎

春秋早期（公元前770年－前7世紀上半葉）

殘高11.8厘米　口徑15.2厘米　腹深6.7厘米　腹徑15厘米　重1019.2克

　　這件鼎的雙耳殘失，口沿經修補成爲現在的無耳樣式。根據鼎的樣式，原來的雙耳應當爲立耳的形式。折沿，口微斂，腹部呈淺半球，體形略顯橫寬，腹部中綫爲最大直徑，並設有一道凸籬形的弦紋。圓底，下接三蹄足，足沿較高，足體內側弧凹。腹部以弦紋爲界，佈置上下兩層不同的龍紋，上飾變形龍紋，每組龍紋兩端爲龍首，體軀作曲折狀，在龍紋的體軀上又飾兩個小鳥紋；下飾兩頭龍紋，龍體作S形，體軀中間有雙首變形鳥紋與之相交，空隙處亦飾小鳥紋。這種龍紋和鳥紋構成的紋飾比較少見。

　　此鼎的造型與河南信陽明港出土的獸體卷曲紋鼎近似[1]，紋飾的佈局也相同。這種鼎沿襲了西周晚期的形制，而紋飾於凸弦紋的上下分佈，則是展現了新的特色。

***Ding* (food vessel) with dragons**

Early Spring and Autumn (770 – first half of the 7th century BC)

Present height 11.8cm, diameter of mouth 15.2cm, depth 6.7cm, diameter of belly 15cm, weight 1019.2g

The wide, shallow *ding* has a hemispherical belly with a round bottom supported by three animal legs. Lacking its handles, the *ding* was restored to the present form. It should originally have two upright handles set on an everted rim. The belly is decorated with two bands of dragons in different forms separated by a raised bow string in the middle. The upper band has stylized dragons with birds; the lower band has sinuous two-headed dragons intertwined with two-headed, stylized birds. These designs featuring dragons and birds are rarely known.

A *ding* decorated with scrolling animals, of similar shape and decorative composition to the current vessel, was unearthed from Minggang, Xinyang, Henan Province (Xinyang 1981b:p.16). This kind of *ding* follows the form of the late Western Zhou period, but displays a new characteristic in its sectional decoration with a raised bow string in the middle of the belly.

1.信陽地區文物管理委員會、信陽縣文化館《信陽縣明港發現兩批春秋早期青銅器》，《中原文物》1981年第4期第16頁。

44

蔡侯鼎

春秋早期（公元前770年－前7世紀上半葉）

高16.9厘米　口徑17.3厘米　腹深8.3厘米　腹徑17厘米　重1794.7克

　　立耳略外撇，方唇折沿，口微斂，腹略鼓，最大腹徑在中綫以下，但並不下垂，器體偏寬。腹底弧度較緩，三蹄形足略向内傾，足部上端飾獸首，並置寬厚的出脊，一足曾斷，於腹部補鑄相接。口沿下飾一周重環紋，腹部飾對稱的卷體龍紋。造型近於河南郟縣太僕鄉春秋墓出土的蟠獸紋鼎[1]。腹部裝飾的龍紋，通常見於鬲的腹部，在鬲腹上皆爲俯首卷體，而於此鼎則作抬首狀。這種對稱的龍紋作爲鼎的裝飾，是十分少見的現象。

　　腹内鑄銘四行16字，其中有數字被修補處所掩：

蔡侯乍（作）宋

姬獎（媵）鼎其

萬年子子孫孫

永寶用享。

　　從銘文可知，此鼎是蔡侯爲蔡國姬姓女子嫁往宋國所鑄的陪嫁器物[2]。蔡侯青銅器多見於春秋晚期，如安徽壽縣蔡侯墓銅器群[3]，在此之前的蔡侯器則僅見於"蔡侯作旅鼎"[4]，時代爲西周晚期，因此，這件鼎爲研究春秋早期的蔡侯青銅器提供了重要資料。

Ding (food vessel) made for Marquis of Cai

Early Spring and Autumn (770 – first half of the 7th century BC)

Height 16.9cm, diameter of mouth 17.3cm, depth 8.3cm, diameter of belly 17cm, weight 1794.7g

The wide _ding_, similar to a _ding_ unearthed from a Spring and Autumn burial at Taipu, Jiaxian, Henan Province (Henan 1954), has two upright handles standing on an everted rim, a slightly bulging belly with a round bottom, as well as three animal legs topped by animal heads with thick flanges. One leg was broken, but has been restored. Under the rim is a band of double oblongs. The belly is decorated with a symmetrical design of dragons with scrolling body, which is commonly seen on _li_ vessels but rare for _ding_ tripods.

A sixteen-character inscription in four columns is cast on the interior of the vessel, which indicates that the _ding_ was made for the Marquis of Cai as a dowry for a girl from a Ji family in his state who would marry a man in the Song State (Cheung Kwong Yue 1997:p.151). Two of the characters are concealed by the remedial restoration.

Most of the bronzes made for the Marquis of Cai are dated from the late Spring and Autumn period, such as those found in Shouxian, Anhui Province (Anhui 1956). A _ding_ with an inscription '_cai hou zuo lü_' of the late Western Zhou gives a rare example of an earlier time (Zhongguo 1986:fig.2441). The current _ding_ provides an important evidence for the research on the bronzes made for the Marquis of Cai in the early Spring and Autumn period.

1.《河南郟縣發現的古代銅器》，《文物參考資料》1954年第3期。

2.參見張光裕《香江新見蔡公子及蔡侯器述略》，《中國文字》新22期第151頁，臺北藝文印書館1997年12月。

3.安徽省文物管理委員會、安徽省博物館《壽縣蔡侯墓出土遺物》，科學出版社1956年版。

4.中國社會科學院考古研究所《殷周金文集成》（第四册）2441，中華書局1986年版。

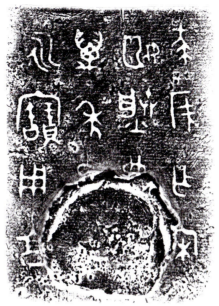

45

秦 公 鼎　　春秋早期（公元前770年－前7世紀上半葉）

高35.2厘米　口徑35.5厘米　腹深14.8厘米　腹徑36厘米　重15200克

此鼎與以下兩件（46、47）形制、紋飾相同，大小相次。口沿外折，上設寬厚大耳，上厚下薄，略爲外侈。束頸，寬體，器腹外垂，淺腹平底，蹄形足。器型頗具西周晚期的氣度。立耳的外側飾鱗紋。頸部和腹部飾不同的獸目交連紋，結構有秦國地域特點。足上部飾獸面紋，有鼻準出脊。整個紋飾風格粗獷、簡約。器內壁鑄銘兩行6字，行款右行：

秦公乍（作）

寶用鼎。

從這三件鼎的形制、紋飾、銘文看，屬同一套列鼎。

獸目交連紋是一種獸紋的變體，在西周晚期和春秋早期的青銅器上大量存在。設置在口沿下的此類紋飾，西周晚期與春秋初期基本沒有差別。這三件秦公鼎口沿下所飾的獸目交連紋均爲兩獸體上下相接，連接處爲一突出的獸目；而腹部的獸目交連紋由兩對雙頭龍紋的變形組合成一組。變形的兩頭龍紋一頭在上，一頭在下稍小。兩對這樣的紋飾尾部上下相接，當中間以獸目，形成完整的一組紋飾。這樣一組紋飾在秦以外的地區尚未有發現，雖然它仍屬於獸目交連紋，但線條較爲複雜，這大概是秦國人力圖模仿西周文化的一種創造性借鑒。

銘文中"秦"字的作"𥠻"，秦，《說文》："𥠻用，伯益之後所封國，地宜禾，從禾舂省。一曰秦，禾名。𥠷，籒文秦，從秝。"段注："地宜禾者，說字形所以從禾從舂也。"朱駿聲《說文通訓定聲》："秦，禾名，從禾從舂省，會意。"籒文、小篆的"秦"字字形均爲從舂省。金文中絕大部分"秦"字的字形都爲從禾舂省，唯有西周恭王時的師西簋秦字未省臼字，作"𥠷"、"𥠻"。雖未省臼，但臼字上下開口，不成全形。此銘文中完全的從舂從雙禾、未省臼字的"秦"字是頗爲少見的。

上海博物館和甘肅省博物館也藏有秦公鼎。上海博物館藏有四件，形制、紋飾與上述二鼎相似，內壁均有銘文，鼎1、鼎2爲"秦公作鑄用鼎"，鼎3、鼎4爲"秦公作寶用鼎"[1]。雖然從銘文看，後兩件與前述三鼎相同，亦爲"秦公作寶用鼎"，但鼎3的行款爲左行，鼎4的行款爲右行，却呈三行排列，因此，這五件銘文相同的秦公鼎，當分屬三套列鼎。甘肅省博物館藏有三件，形制、紋飾相同，口沿下飾獸目交連紋，腹部飾三排相錯的垂鱗紋，內壁鑄銘兩行6字："秦公作鑄用鼎"[2]。

20世紀90年代，在甘肅禮縣大堡子山發現早期秦公陵墓，其中有2號墓、3號墓兩座大墓。據研究，上述秦公鼎以及其他一些器物即出自這兩座大墓，這些器物的形制、紋飾、組合等方面都表現西周末至春秋初的特點，銘文中的"秦公"應當不出秦襄公或文公的範圍[3]。據《史記·秦本紀》記載，秦襄公因護送周平王東遷有功，被分封爲諸侯。有關反映秦國早期歷史的文獻記載和考古數據很少，因此，這三件秦公鼎具有重要的歷史價值。

1.李朝遠《上海博物館新獲秦公器研究》，《上海博物館集刊》第七期，上海書畫出版社1996年版。

2.禮縣博物館、禮縣秦西垂文化研究會《秦西垂陵區》第12頁，文物出版社2004年版。

3.參見禮縣博物館、禮縣秦西垂文化研究會《秦西垂陵區》第12頁。

Ding (food vessel) made for Duke of Qin

Early Spring and Autumn (770 – first half of the 7th century BC)
Height: 35.2cm, diameter of mouth 35.5cm, depth 14.8cm, diameter of belly 36cm, weight 15200g

This *ding* and the following two tripods (pls. 46 and 47), identical in style and decoration, vary slightly in size. Two sturdy oblique handles rise from the everted mouth rim. The wide belly with flat bottom rests on three hoof-shaped legs. This is a typical style of the late Western Zhou. Scaly pattern decorates the outside of the handles. On their necks and bellies are different patterns of *shoumu jiaolian* (animals connected by the eyes), characteristic of the Qin State. Animal masks on the legs have flanged noses. The overall decoration is simple and crude. A double-column six-character inscription is cast on the inside of each vessel, reading '*Qin Gong zuo bao yong ding* (A precious *ding* made for the Duke of Qin)'. Based on the shape, decoration and inscription, these three vessels should be in one set.

Pattern of *shoumu jiaolian* is a kind of stylized animal design, which appear most frequently on the bronzes from the late Western Zhou to the early Spring and Autumn periods. The animals below the rim of these *ding* tripods are arranged in pairs, with the upper and the lower one joined by a protruding eye; and this pattern of the late Western Zhou did not experience much change in the early Spring and Autumn period. On the other hand, the pattern on the belly featuring two double-head dragons connected together with one eye in the middle was not known in areas outside the Qin State. This complicate design should be a creation of the Qin people on the basis of Western Zhou culture.

The *qin* character in the inscription, constructed in the form of '![qin character]', is very atypicall and rarely seen.

In the collections of the Shanghai Museum and the Gansu Provincial Museum are also tripods made for the Duke of Qin. The four pieces in the Shanghai Museum are the same as these three exhibits in shape and decoration; two of them have the inscription of '*Ding* cast for the Duke of Qin' and the other two have the inscription of 'A precious *ding* made for the Duke of Qin' (Li Chaoyuan 1996). Although the latter two have the same inscription as these three pieces, the five items belong to three different sets. Only one of the inscriptions reads from the right to the left, and the rests the other way round. Besides, the examples from the Shanghai Museum have three-column inscriptions instead of two-column ones. The three tripods in the Gansu Provincial Museum have the pattern of *shoumu jiaolian* on the neck, but scaly pattern on the belly. Six characters in two columns reading '*Qin Gong zuo zhu yong ding* (*Ding* cast for the Duke of Qin)' can be found on the interior (Lixian 2004, p.12).

In the 1990's, a burial of the Duke of Qin was discovered in the Dabuzi Mountain, Lixian, Gansu Province. It is concluded that these tripods and some other objects are from the burials M2 and M3, the shape, decoration and design of which are characteristic of the late Western Zhou and the early Spring and Autumn periods. The Duke of Qin (*Qin Gong*) in the inscriptions should be either Duke Xiang or Duke Wen of Qin (Lixian 2004, p.12). It is recorded in *Shiji* (Records of the Grand Historian) that a dukedom was conferred upon Duke Xiang of Qin after he had escorted King Ping of the Zhou dynasty to the east. In view of the rare written and archaeological materials on the history of the early Qin period, these three tripods made for the Duke of Qin are very important to the study of this area.

秦 公 鼎

春秋早期（公元前770年－前7世紀上半葉）

高32.4厘米　口徑33厘米　腹深14.3厘米　腹徑31.8厘米　重12920克

***Ding* (food vessel) made for Duke of Qin**

Early Spring and Autumn (770 – first half of the 7th century BC)

Height 32.4cm, diameter of mouth 33cm, depth 14.3cm, diameter of belly 31.8cm, weight 12920g

133

秦 公 鼎 春秋早期（公元前770年 – 前7世纪上半葉）

高30.5厘米　口徑31厘米　腹深13.5厘米　腹徑31.7厘米　重11250克

***Ding* (food vessel)
made for Duke of Qin**

Early Spring and Autumn (770 – first half of the 7th century BC)

Height 30.5cm, diameter of mouth 31cm, depth 13.5cm, diameter of belly 31.7cm, weight 11250g

秦公簋　春秋早期（公元前770年－前7世紀上半葉）
高16.4厘米　口徑18.7厘米　腹深9.7厘米　腹徑24.5厘米　重5200克

此簋與下一件簋（49）形制、紋飾基本相同。失蓋，弇口，體寬鼓腹，圈足下接三獸足，下連短狀獸爪形矮扁足。腹部兩側設獸首形耳，造型宏偉，耳端龍首寬厚，卷身，下有垂珥呈卷尾狀。口沿下飾獸目交連紋，腹部飾三層交錯的垂鱗紋，圈足上飾一周鱗紋。器內底鑄銘兩行6字：

秦公乍（作）

鑄用簋。

銘文中"鑄"字作"鑄"和"鑄"，鑄，《說文》："鑄，銷金也。從金，壽聲"，壽從𤔩聲，𤔩從𠤳聲[1]。金文中的鑄字，最完整的字形作鑄，從彐從鬲從金從火從皿，𠤳聲，像手持鬲形蓋以火銷金於爐橐形。這兩件簋銘中的鑄字，前者從彐、從鬲、從皿，字𠤳，省金、省火；後者從鬲、從皿、𠤳聲，省金、省彐、省火。特別是兩字的皿下缺一筆，這是比較少見的現象。

兩件簋的紋飾與甘肅禮縣大堡子山秦公陵墓的2號墓、3號墓兩座大墓所出的垂鱗紋秦公鼎相近[2]，均爲口沿下飾獸目交連紋，腹部飾三重垂鱗紋，因此也爲大堡子山秦公陵墓所出，但兩者的銘文風格有所不同。

上海博物館也收藏有兩件秦公簋，形制與這兩件相近，蓋沿和口沿下的紋飾均爲獸目交連紋，且上下相對，每組紋飾皆間飾浮雕狀獸首，蓋沿八個，器沿六個，上下口口相對。蓋面和器腹紋飾均爲橫條溝紋。器、蓋對銘各有兩行5字："秦公乍寶簋"[3]。顯然，這兩件簋與上述兩件簋，屬於不同的銅器組合。

Gui (food vessel) made for Duke of Qin

Early Spring and Autumn (770 – first half of the 7th century BC)
Height 16.4cm, diameter of mouth 18.7cm, depth 9.7cm, diameter of belly 24.5cm, weight 5200g

This *gui* and the following vessel, identical in shape and decoration, have lost their lids. Each has a drum-shaped bowl standing on a foot-ring supported by three claw-like feet. The two curve handles are surmounted by animal heads in relief, and carry appendages in the form of curling tails. Around the neck runs the stylized pattern of *shoumu jiaolian* (animals connected by the eyes). Scaly pattern decorates the exterior in three interlocking sections and covers the foot-ring. There is an inscription of six characters in two columns on the interior, reading 'Qin Gong zuo zhu yong gui ([A vessel] cast for the Duke of Qin)'. The character of *zhu*, or cast, on these two vessels is rarely known in bronze inscriptions (Chou Fa-kao 1975, vol.14, p.7569).

The decoration of these two vessels is similar to that of the tripods from the burials M2 and M3 of the Duke of Qin's burial in the Dabaozi Mountain, Lixian, Gansu Province (Lixian 2004, p.12). They are all decorated with the pattern of *shoumu jiaolian* below the mouth rim and three sections of scales on the body. These two vessels should belong to the same Qin burial in Dabaozi Mountain; however, the style of inscription is not the same.

1.周法高主編《金文詁林》第十四冊第7569頁引高田忠周語，香港中文大學1975年版。

2.禮縣博物館、禮縣秦西垂文化研究會《秦西垂陵區》第12頁，文物出版社2004年版。

3.李朝遠《上海博物館新獲秦公器研究》，《上海博物館集刊》第七期，上海書畫出版社1996年版

Two other *gui* made for the Duke of Qin and of similar shape to these present examples are in the Shanghai Museum Colletion. The pattern around both the lid and the mouth is *shoumu jiaolian*, separated by relief animal heads with eight on the lid and six under the mouth. In addition, there are horizontal grooves on the lid and the body. Both the lid and the bowl are cast with a five-character inscription in two columns, reading '*Qin Gong zuo bao gui* (A precious vessel made for the Duke of Qin)' (Li Chaoyuan 1996). Obviously, these vessels do not belong to the same group of bronzes as the exhibits.

49

秦公簋 | 春秋早期（公元前770年－前7世紀上半葉）
高16.2厘米　口徑18.9厘米　腹深9.2厘米　腹徑22.8厘米　重4471.3克

Gui (food vessel)
made for Duke of Qin | Early Spring and Autumn (770 – first half of the 7th century BC)
Height 16.2cm, diameter of mouth 18.9cm, depth 9.2cm, diameter of belly 22.8cm, weight 4471.3g

50

垂鱗紋鍑

春秋早期（公元前770年－前7世紀上半葉）

通高22.1厘米　口徑18.8厘米　腹深14.2厘米　腹徑17.1厘米　重2999.6克

直口，方唇，深腹，腹壁略微斜收，喇叭形高圈足。口沿兩側設有絢索紋立耳，耳的內根部呈蛇頭狀，緊貼於器口的內緣。口沿下裝飾一周獸目交連紋，腹部裝飾雙層垂鱗紋，兩圈紋飾之間以一條凸起的絢紋爲界。這件鍑上的獸目交連紋，據目前的資料尚不見於西周時期的青銅器，而與上海博物館所藏秦公鼎2、秦公鼎4口沿下的紋飾十分相似[1]，秦公鼎爲春秋早期的器物。

與這件器物相似者，目前還發現有四件：垂鱗紋鍑（上海博物館藏）[2]，絢索紋立耳的外根部呈蛇頭狀，並緊貼於器口的外緣；垂鱗紋鍑（甘肅省博物館藏）[3]，獸目交連紋和垂鱗紋之間爲一周凸起的弦紋；波曲紋鍑（上海博物館藏，1994年范季融先生捐贈）[4]，口沿下飾獸目交連的雙首龍紋，體軀方折，中間爲目紋，兩端各有一個回顧龍首，腹部飾波曲紋；波曲紋鍑（加拿大多倫多皇家安大略博物館藏）[5]，其索紋立耳的外根部呈蛇頭狀，並緊貼於器沿的外側。獸目交連紋的目紋在紋飾長邊的中間。

這五件鍑的器形與秦公諸器有西周晚期的氣度，卻無西周器之精緻的狀況十分相象，而所有的紋飾均較爲粗獷，體現了秦國的風格特點。從紋飾和甘肅禮縣秦公墓其他器物的綜合判斷，屬於春秋早期偏早的秦國青銅器，即爲秦式鍑。秦式鍑是在兩周之交時，出現於開始融入并挺進中原文化圈的西陲，在歷史舞臺上短暫逗留之後，又伴隨着秦的東進，秦式鍑也漸次向東發展，從今天的甘肅往陝西，再折向北進入山西、河北，迅速與中原文化激蕩交融，最後在春秋戰國之交時，受三晉文化的浸潤而逐漸淡出。而在秦式鍑向東發展的同時，北方草原鍑出現了自己的發展軌迹。它們也可能有共同的祖源，之後是多元的非綫形的各自發展[6]。

***Fu* (food vessel) with scale pattern**

Early Spring and Autumn (770 – first half of the 7th century BC)
Height 22.1cm, diameter of mouth 18.8cm, depth 14.2cm, diameter of belly 17.1cm, weight 2999.6g

This vessel has a deep bowl resting on a high conical foot-ring. Two rope handles with snake head ends are set on the mouth rim. Below the mouth rim runs a band of *shoumu jiaolian* (animals connected by the eyes) and, the belly below a raised band of rope pattern is decorated with a double layer of scales. This kind of *shoumu jiaolian* pattern, never been found on bronzes of the Western Zhou period, is similar to that of two *ding* (2 and 4) made for the Duke of Qin of the early Spring and Autumn period from the Shanghai Museum (Li Chaoyuan 1996).

Four other vessels similar to this *fu* are known. One in the Shanghai Museum (Li Chaoyuan 2004) and the one in the Gansu Provincial Museum (Li Yongping 1999; Li Yongping 2000) are decorated with scale pattern. The third one, again in the Shanghai Museum and a gift

---

1.李朝遠《上海博物館新獲秦公器研究》，《上海博物館集刊》第七期，上海書畫出版社1996年版。

2.李朝遠《新見秦式青銅鍑的研究》，《文物》2004年第1期。

3.李永平《新見秦公墓文物及相關問題探識》，臺北《故宮文物月刊》1999年五月號；《甘肅省博物館系統所藏青銅器選介》，《文物》2000年第12期第70頁。

4.同2

5.同2

6.參見李朝遠《新見秦式青銅鍑的研究》。

of Mr. George Fan (Li Chaoyuan 2004), and the fourth one in the Royal Ontario Museum, Toronto, Canada (Li Chaoyuan 2004) are decorated with wave pattern.

All these five *fu*, and the vessels made for the Duke of Qin alike, are modeled on late Western Zhou bronzes, however, they lack the fineness of the latter but embody the crudity typical of bronzes from the Qin State. Judging from its decoration, which is similar to that of the bronzes from the Duke of Qin's burial in Lixian, Gansu Province, this piece belongs to Qin bronzes of the very early Spring and Autumn period. This Qin style *fu* appeared in the western region (modern day Gansu) between the Western and the Eastern Zhou period, and was brought to Shaanxi, Shanxi, and Hebei regions as the Qin power moved eastwards. It eventually disappeared between the Spring and Autumn and the Warring States periods. Besides, the contemporaneous *fu* of the northern nomads might have the same origin as the Qin style *fu* though they developed separately (Li Chaoyuan 2004).

51

鳥龍紋匜

春秋早期（公元前770年－前7世紀上半葉）

高16.6厘米　流至口長32厘米　腹深8.3厘米　重2975.2克

　　器腹作長橢圓的瓢形，口緣漸升，寬流昂起，流口後傾，深腹圓底，下設四條獸爪形扁足，後部龍形鋬從下蜿蜒而上，龍吻銜口沿，拱體卷尾，頗具動感。腹部中間飾瓦棱紋，口沿下和近底部以及四足飾交龍紋，交龍紋以雙綫組成，體軀方折，在一些轉角處置有一目，以示龍首所在，紋飾風格粗疏。甘肅禮縣圓頂山發現的秦貴族墓地中所出鼎、簋也有此類交龍紋[1]。口沿下的交龍紋中還夾飾以鳥紋，鳥爲側面形象，尖喙，圓眼，體態小巧，羽翼清晰可辨，一正一倒連續的排列。如此的交龍紋和鳥紋的紋飾組合非常罕見。這件匜的形制和紋飾所反映出的特點體現了較爲明顯的秦器風格[2]。

　　匜是注水器。商周時期祭祀和宴饗前要先舉行沃盥之禮，即净手之禮，需用匜澆水於手，盤則是用來承接棄水的。匜是西周中期才出現的水器，在此之前，是盉與盤形成組合作爲沃盥禮時的用具。現在所知最早的一件匜，是1975年陝西岐山縣董家村1號青銅器窖藏中出土的憮匜，在它的銘文中還是自稱爲盉[3]。由此可見，匜是由盉的功能演化而來的一種新的水器器形。

_Yi_ (water vessel) with birds and dragons

Early Spring and Autumn (770 – first half of the 7th century BC)

Height 16.6cm, length 32cm, depth 8.3cm, weight 2975.2g

This ladle-shaped vessel has a dragon handle and four claw-shaped feet. Intertwined dragons of raised double string appear below the rim, on the belly and the feet. Dragon eyes seen at the corners represent dragon heads. Similar dragon designs have been found on the _ding_ and _gui_ from the noble burials of the Qin State in Yuanding Mountain, Lixian, Gansu Province (Lixian 2004, pls. 12-15,17 and 29). Alongside the intertwined dragons appearing below the rim are small birds in profile with sharp beak, round eyes and clearly depicted feathers. Such a design with dragons and birds is very rare, and the present _yi_ shows characteristics of Qin bronzes (Chen Ping 1984).

Water was poured from a _yi_ for washing hands before rituals and banquets in the Shang and Zhou periods while a water bowl called _pan_ was used to catch the water. As the _yi_ vessel did not appeared until the mid Western Zhou period, the _he_ vessel was used instead. The earliest _yi_ known is the '憮 _yi_' found from the No.1 bronze hoard in Dongjiacun of Qishan County, Shaanxi Province; however, it is still labeled a _he_ in the inscription on the vessel (Pang Huaiqing 1976:p.26). Hence, _yi_ is apparently a new type of water vessel developing from _he_.

1.禮縣博物館、禮縣秦西垂文化研究會《秦西垂陵區》圖版貳九、一二至一五、一七，文物出版社2004年版。

2.參見陳平《試論關中秦墓青銅容器的分期問題》，《考古與文物》1984年第3期第58頁、第4期第63頁。

3.龐懷清等《陝西省岐山縣董家村西周銅器窖穴發掘簡報》，《文物》1976年第5期第26頁。

52

子范鬲　春秋中期（公元前7世紀上半葉－前6世紀上半葉）
高10.9厘米　口徑14.7厘米　腹深6.9厘米　腹徑13.3厘米　重1115克

　　口沿較寬，平折，短直束頸，圓肩，鼓腹寬襠，三獸蹄足，足內側較平。器身置有三道出脊。腹部飾龍紋，這種龍紋以寬綫條構成，略帶有方折，體軀卷曲，共有四個龍紋構成一組，中間兩個角與角彎曲相連，兩側的龍紋爲倒置，角與中間龍紋的吻部銜接，構圖頗爲獨特。通常這種款式的鬲多飾兩兩相對的卷尾龍紋，因此，這是比較少見的情形。

　　口沿鑄有銘文：

　　子範（犯）之寶鬲（鬲）。

　　子范亦見於子范編鐘¹，子范鬲銘文中“范”字作“𨊰”，而子范編鐘銘文作“𨊰”，兩者的寫法有所不同，《殷周金文集成》所錄一件鼎上也作“𡴭”²。據《左傳》、《史記》，晉文公之舅狐偃，其字爲子范。子范編鐘銘文記載子范一生中曾輔佐晉文公返晉復國、城濮之戰、踐土之盟等三件大事。

***Li* (food vessel) made for Zifan**

Mid Spring and Autumn (first half of the 7th century – first half of the 6th century BC)
Height 10.9cm, diameter of mouth 14.7cm, depth 6.9cm, diameter of belly 13.3cm, weight 1115g

This tripod has a wide and flat mouth rim, a short and slender neck, a bulging belly and three hoof-shaped legs. Between the three flanges on the belly are dragon designs, each comprising four dragons: two in middle with their horns interlocked, the other two are upside down and their horns are connected with the former's mouths. This dragon design is atypical for the *li*, which is mostly decorated with two pairs of dragons with coiling tails facing each other.

On the mouth rim is an inscription, reading 'Zifan zhi bao li (A precious li made for Zifan)'. Similar inscriptions also appear on bell chimes made for Zifan (Chang Kuang-yuan 1995:p.4). The *fan* character on this vessel '𨊰' is different from that of the bell chimes '𨊰'. The same character '𡴭' is seen on a *ding* recorded in *Yin Zhou jinwen jicheng* (Zhongguo 1986:fig.2104). It is recorded in *Zuozhuan* (Zuo Qiuming's Commentary on the Spring and Autumn Annals) and *Shiji* (Records of the Grand Historian) that Zifan is the style name of Huyan, uncle of Duke Wen of Jin. The inscriptions on the bell chimes record three great events participated by Zifan in support of Duke Wen, including regaining control of the Jin State, the war of Chengpu, and the alliance of Jiantu.

1.張光遠《春秋晉文公稱霸“子范編鐘”初釋》，臺北《故宮文物月刊》13卷1期（總145）第4頁，1995年4月。
2.中國社會科學院考古研究所《殷周金文集成》（第四冊）2104，中華書局1986年版。

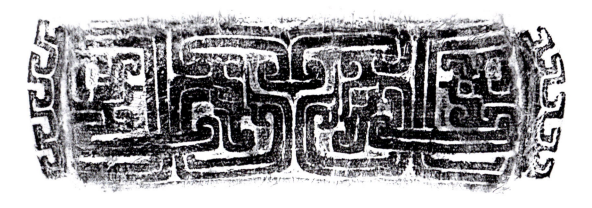

145

53

蟠龍紋盆 | 春秋晚期（公元前6世紀上半葉－前476年）
高13.9厘米　口徑26.9厘米　腹深13.2厘米　腹徑29厘米　重2879.9克

　　折沿，束頸，折肩，肩、腹連接處爲最大的腹徑，然後腹壁下斂，平底。肩兩側有獸首半環耳，獸角螺旋狀盤起成爲錐形。口沿下和腹部裝飾蟠龍紋，每個蟠龍紋曲折而彎，以頸部和體軀相連，肩部爲一周絢紋。此盆的形制、紋飾與河南淅川下寺2號墓出土的一件盆（M2:68）相似[1]，此墓墓主是王子午，爲楚康王時的令尹，卒於魯襄公二十一年（公元前522），因此該墓的年代爲春秋晚期前段[2]，而盆的年代也與之相當。傳世的曾大保盆與上述二盆較爲相似，其銘文中自名爲"盆"[3]、息子行飪盆[4]、黃太子伯克醈盆[5]、郎子宿車行盆[6]、樊君盆[7]等也自名爲盆，曾、息、黃、樊諸國皆在江、淮間，"盆"可能是當地對此類器物的一種稱呼；而《周金文存》所錄的晉公盞則自名爲"盞"，這當爲江、淮以外地區的名稱。

　　盆可用於盛水，也可盛放食物，《儀禮·士喪禮》："新盆，盤，瓶，廢敦，重鬲，皆濯造於西階下"，鄭玄注："盆以盛水"；《周禮·地官·牛人》："凡祭祀共其牛牲之互，與其盆簝以待事"，鄭玄注："盆所以盛血"。子諆盆自名爲"盂"[8]，説明盆的功能與盂相近，而盂主要也是盛水、放食物的器具，但盆銘中的"飪盆"、"醈盆"、"行盆"則表明了其主要用途是盛放食物。

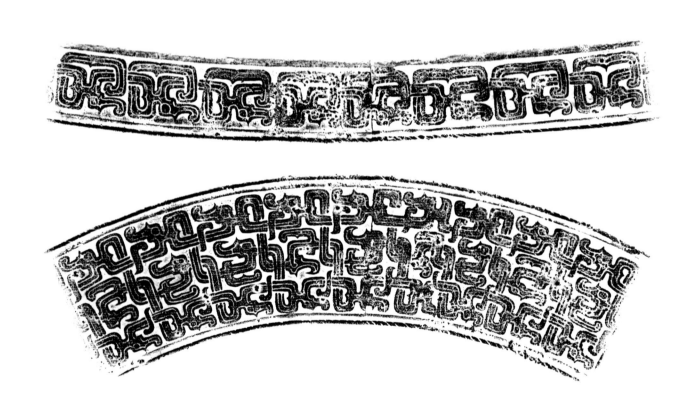

1.河南省文物研究所等《淅川下寺春秋楚墓》第136頁，文物出版社1991年版。
2.同上第318頁。
3.容庚《商周彝器通考》圖版八八〇，哈佛燕京學社1941年版。
4.程欣人《隨縣溳陽出土楚、曾、息青銅器》，《江漢考古》1980年第1期第97頁。
5.山東省文物考古研究所、沂水縣文物管理站《山東沂水劉家店子春秋墓發掘簡報》，《文物》1984年第9期第1頁。
6.信陽地區文物管理委員會、羅山縣文化館《羅山縣高店公社又發現一批春秋時期青銅器》，《中原文物》1981年第4期第18頁。
7.河南省博物館等《河南信陽市平橋春秋墓發掘簡報》，《文物》1981年第1期第9頁。
8.信陽地區文物管理委員會、潢川縣文化館《河南潢川縣發現黃國和蔡國銅器》，《文物》1980年第1期第46頁。

Pen (water or food vessel) with coiling dragons

Late Spring and Autumn (first half of the 6th century – 476 BC)
Height 13.9cm, diameter of mouth 26.9cm, depth 13.2cm, diameter of belly 29cm, weight 2879.9g

This bowl has an everted rim, a waisted neck, angular shoulders, and the body tapers down to a flat bottom. Two handles with animal heads are set on the sides. Coiling dragons appear below the mouth rim and on the belly, separated by rope pattern on the shoulder. The style and decoration of this vessel are similar to a *pen* excavated from a burial (M2:68) at Xiasi, Xichuan County, Henan Province (Henan 1991:p.136). It was the burial of Wang Ziwu, the highest official (*Lingyin*) of King Kang of the Chu State, who died in 552 BC. Thus, this vessel should be dated to the late Spring and Autumn period (Henan 1991:p.318). Besides, these two vessels are quite similar to a *pen* made for Zeng Dabao, which is labeled as a '*pen*' in the inscription (Rong Geng 1941:pl.880). Four more examples being labeled '*pen*' in the inscriptions are known, the Xi Zi Xing Si *pen* (Chen Xinren 1980:p.97), Huang Taizi Boke 餗 *pen* (Shandong 1984:p.1), 鄑 Zi Shu Che Xing *pen* (Xinyang 1981a:p.18) and Fan Jun *pen* (Henan 1981:p.9) from the states of Zeng, Xi, Huang and Chu. *Pen*, referring to this type of vessel, was probably a widely adopted term in the area between the Yangtze River and the Huai River. On the other hand, as recorded in *Zhou jinwen cun* (Records of Inscription on Bronzes of Zhou Dynasty) a *pen* made for Jin Gong was labeled a '盨', showing that the same type of vessel was named differently outside the region of the Yangtze and the Huai River.

Pen is used to contain water and food. In Zheng Xuan's commentary to *Yili* (Ritual Manual), *pen* is used to contain water, while in Zheng's commentary to *Zhouli* (Ritual of Zhou), *pen* is used for holding blood. A *pen* made for Zi Qi is labeled as a *yu* (Xinyang 1980:p.46), which is a vessel for containing water and food. For other examples labeled as '*si pen*', '餗 *pen*', and '*xing pen*' in the inscriptions, they are generally used to contain food.

54

交龍紋甗　春秋晚期（公元前6世紀上半葉－前476年）
高45厘米　口徑30.6厘米　重7000克

　　甑、鬲分體式甗。甑直口折沿，束頸，略有斜肩，寬體深腹，腹壁弧曲，圈足。頸部兩側設附耳，其內側下端有兩根小橫樑與頸部相連。鬲體呈圓罐狀，侈口，束頸，器腹扁圓，圓底下接三蹄足，肩兩側置外傾的立耳，亦有兩根小橫樑與頸部相連。底部與柱足有明顯的煙炱痕迹。甑的頸部飾交龍紋，腹上部爲一周凸起的絢紋，其下爲交龍紋和三角雲紋，耳外側亦飾交龍紋。鬲腹飾兩道弦紋。這件甗的甑部寬大，鬲部呈扁矮的罐體，且上下連接的方法爲甑足插入鬲口，這是比較少見的情形。

　　甗是蒸炊器，主要是用來蒸煮飯食，甑部用於放置糧食，鬲用於盛水，中間有箅相隔，箅上有十字形或直條形鏤孔，以通蒸汽，鬲下可以舉火煮水，以蒸汽蒸炊食物。商代晚期和西周早期皆爲聯體甗，至西周中期以後，甗的器形才有比較大的變化，出現了方甗，以及甑和鬲分體的式樣。

Yan (food vessel) with intertwined dragons

Late Spring and Autumn (first half of the 6th century – 476 BC)
Height 45cm, diameter of mouth 30.6cm, weight 7000g

This _yan_ is made up of two parts: the upper part is a _zeng_ with an everted rim and a deep bowl resting on a foot-ring, and the lower part is a _li_ in the shape of a round jar with an everted rim and a convex bottom supported by three hoof-like legs. Traces of being heated over fire can be seen on the bottom and the legs. Both pieces have two handles. The _zeng_ has intertwined dragons on the neck and dragons with triangular clouds appear on the belly below a raised band of rope pattern. The handles are also decorated with intertwined dragons. The _li_ has simply two raised strings. This _yan_ is unusual in having such a big _zeng_ being inserted into the compressed _li_.

Yan is a vessel used for cooking food in the steam. Food is put in the _zeng_ and water in the _li_. In between the two parts is a _bi_, i.e. a grate with square or horizontal openings allowing steam to pass through. _Yan_ of the late Shang to the early Western Zhou period was a one-piece vessel, while the two-piece _yan_ and square ones appeared in the mid Western Zhou period.

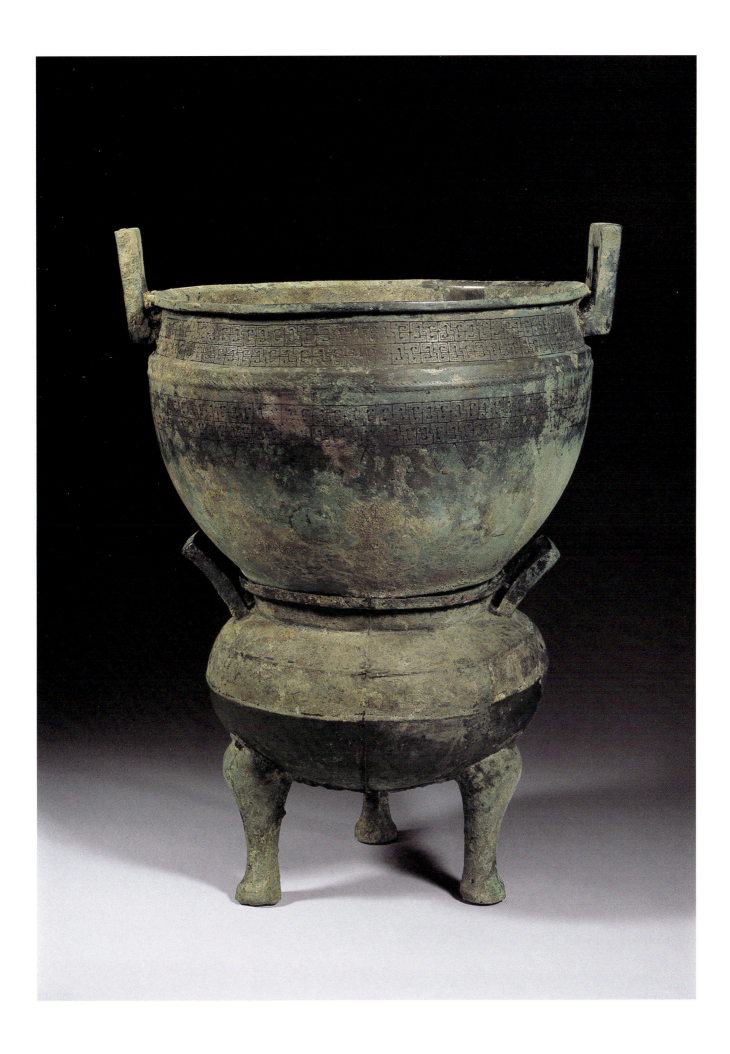

55

蟠蛇紋豆

春秋晚期（公元前6世紀上半葉－前476年）
高21.5厘米　口徑16.7厘米　腹深9.4厘米　腹徑17.7厘米　重1847.5克

　　這件豆帶有淺弧蓋，上有盤形短柄的捉手，蓋口罩在器的子口外，取下後卻置即可成爲一個食盤。器身直口，腹部弧形斜收爲圓底，下接高足圓盤柄，柄上段垂直，下段外撇爲盤形圈足。腹部兩側設置對稱的寬環形耳。其形制與山西侯馬上馬墓地1002號墓出土的銅豆相近[1]。蓋頂的捉手內和圈足上裝飾龍紋，蓋面飾蟠蛇紋兩周，中間以寬條紋爲界，器腹亦飾蟠蛇紋，腹部中央有一周凸起的絢紋，下端飾以蟠蛇紋組成的垂葉紋。此器裝飾的蟠蛇紋，實際上是一種細緻密集的龍紋排列，龍紋通過微縮變形，通常殘留有小小的圈點紋，表現了龍首和眼睛，這些複雜的紋飾綫條按照一定規律排列，成爲一個個紋飾方塊。前述上馬墓地1002號墓銅豆飾有這種紋飾，山西侯馬鑄銅作坊遺址也出土過不少相同紋飾的陶範和陶模[2]。從造型和紋飾看，這件豆具有晉系青銅器的風格特徵。

　　按照先秦文獻的記載，豆主要是盛放腌菜、肉醬等調味品的器具。豆在商代晚期已經使用，但數量很少。直至春秋戰國時期才較爲盛行，成爲青銅禮器中常見的組合器物之一，這時豆的用途可能有一些改變，洛陽燒溝戰國墓出土的一些陶蓋豆中，還留有粟米的遺存。研究表明，這種豆的功用與簋、敦有相似之處，也可用作盛放黍、稷、稻、粱類的飯食[3]。

***Dou* (food vessel) with serpentines**

Late Spring and Autumn (first half of the 6th century – 476 BC)
Height 21.5cm, diameter of mouth 16.7cm, depth 9.4cm, diameter of belly 17.7cm, weight 1847.5g

This high-foot bowl has a convex lid, which can be used as a dish when taken off. The round body and bottom stands on a trumpet-shaped stem. Two loop handles are attached to the sides of the belly. A *dou* of similar shape was unearthed from the burial M1002 in Shangma graveyard, Houma, Shanxi Province (Shanxi 1994:pl.44). Dragons decorate the lid handle and the foot-ring, while coiled serpentines (*panshe*) appear on the lid and the body with a raised band of rope pattern. Pendant leaves formed by coiled serpentines decorate the lower body. The pattern of *panshe* is a myriad of stylized dragons represented by circles, which symbolize dragon heads and eyes. The *dou* from Shangma is also cast with this pattern, in addition, many clay models and moulds with the *panshe* pattern have been recovered from the sites of bronze foundries in Houma, Shanxi province (Shanxi 1996a:pls.637-657). Judging by the shape and decoration, this *dou* is reminiscent of the bronzes from the Jin State.

As recorded in historical texts, *dou* was used mainly for containing various pickles and minced meat. It appeared in the late Shang period, but became popular much later on in the Spring and Autumn to the Warring States period, when it was included as part of the ritual bronze set. The function of *dou* might have changed at this time. Some pottery *dou* excavated from Warring States burials in Shaogou, Luoyang contain maize residues. Like *gui* and *dui*, *dou* was then used to contain cereals including maize and rice (Gao Ming 1981).

1.山西省考古研究所《上馬墓地》圖版44，文物出版社1994年版。

2.山西省考古研究所《侯馬陶範藝術》圖版637－657，美國普林斯敦大學出版社1996年版。

3.高明《中原地區東周時代青銅器研究（中）》，《考古與文物》1981年第3期。

56

鷹獸紋戚　春秋晚期（公元前6世紀上半葉－前476年）
高8.6厘米　長12.9厘米　重285克

　　援呈長方體，無刃，前端稍寬並分歧，上飾兩層龍紋，由陰綫構成。援之後部浮雕一獸，頭有後卷角，小耳，口部咬住援的上沿，體軀躬曲，雙爪捧持援的兩面，其後有一鷹，與之合體，鷹的尖喙銜住一條蛇，蛇體扭動掙扎。鷹、獸的體軀滿飾不規則六角形構成的點粒紋，而鷹翅由鱗紋組成。銎呈扁圓形，中間有對穿的小圓孔，下部設一圈飾有絢紋凸箍，銎内殘存有柲木。德國柏林東亞藝術博物館藏有一件戚與之造型、紋飾相同[1]。這類方援的青銅戚比較少見，山東臨沂鳳凰山春秋晚期墓曾出土一件[2]，援爲長方體，銎的上部爲鳳首形，口銜長援，兩者形制相似，而鷹銜蛇的形象與侯馬出土陶範上蟠龍銜蛇的紋飾比較近同[3]。

　　這件戚造型獨特，紋飾奇異，整體鑄作精美，從臨沂鳳凰山墓爲諸侯國國君之墓來看[4]，此類器物當爲象徵王權的禮器。

_Qi_ (axe) with an eagle and a mythical animal

Late Spring and Autumn (first half of the 6th century – 476 BC)
Height 8.6cm, length 12.9cm, weight 285g

This axe has a rectangular blade without a cutting edge, and its bifurcated end is decorated with two layers of dragons in sunken lines. Another end of the blade is adorned with an openwork mythical animal with coiling horn on the head, and clasping the blade with its two claws. On the back of it, an eagle is biting a struggling snake. Many hexagonal spots were arranged on the bodies of eagle and animal, while the wings of eagle are decorated with scale pattern. The oval shaft of the axe is hollow with some remains of the original wood half of the axe inside. A similar axe is in the collection of the Museum fur Ostasiatische Kunst, Berlin, Germany (Li Xueqin and Sarah Allan 1995:pl.129). This kind of axe with a rectangular blade is rare. One with a phoenix end was excavated from a late Spring and Autumn burial in Fenghuang Mountain, Linyi, Shandong Province (Shandong 1987:p.29). The pattern of an eagle biting snake is similar to that of *pan* dragons and snakes on clay moulds from Houma (Shanxi 1993:vol.1, pp.225-228).

This axe has an unusual shape, with grotesque pattern, and delicate casting technique, indicating that it was a symbol of status for a king of a feudal state as witnessed by the piece from Fenghuang Mountain (Shandong 1987:p.35).

1. 李學勤、艾蘭《歐洲所藏中國青銅器遺珠》圖版129，文物出版社1995年版。
2. 山東省兖石鐵路文物考古工作隊《臨沂鳳凰山東周墓》第29頁，齊魯書社1987年版。
3. 山西省考古研究所《侯馬鑄銅遺址》（上册）第225至228頁，文物出版社1993年版。
4. 山東省兖石鐵路文物考古工作隊《臨沂鳳凰山東周墓》第35頁。

57

鳥紋戈 春秋晚期（公元前6世紀上半葉－前476年）
高8.6厘米　長13.2厘米

　　短援作三角形，援末下垂成胡，刃部較爲鋒利。胡後有橢圓形銎，內中留有柲木，近銎口有一周凸箍，中部設對穿小圓孔，用於固定戈柲。銎上部裝飾一鳥，鳥首曲昂，圓目，鉤形尖喙，頸飾鱗紋，鳥身羽毛豐滿，雙翅微張，長尾上下分歧。雙爪貼於銎壁，並緊攫扭動的一條蛇，蛇呈雙身形，蛇首向下，在銎的後側，這種雙身蛇表現的是蛇體的兩個側面，爲青銅器中常用的紋飾佈局方法。

　　此戈造型、紋飾與洛陽中州路春秋晚期墓出土的1式戈基本相同[1]；也近於山西侯馬出土的一件戈範，除造型外，兩者所飾的鳥紋風格也比較近似[2]；類似的鳥紋見於太原金勝村所出的Ⅱ式戈、Ⅰ式鐏[3]以及侯馬陶範[4]；相似的蛇紋在侯馬陶範中亦有發現[5]。這件戈屬於周王畿或晉系青銅器。

***Ge* (dagger-axe) with a bird**

Late Spring and Autumn (first half of the 6th century – 476 BC)
Height 8.6cm, length 13.2cm

This *ge* has a short triangle blade with a sharp edge and an oval joint with two holes to fix it onto a shaft, in fact, residues of a wood shaft remain in the joint. Set atop is a bird with an uplifted head, round eyes, hook beak, scales on the neck, slightly stretched wings and a bifurcated tail. Its claws are clutching a struggling snake. The twofold body represents the two sides of it, which is a popular representation seen on bronzes.

The shape and design of this *ge* are basically the same as a *ge* (Type I) excavated from a late Spring and Autumn burial at Zhongzhou Road, Luoyang (Luoyang 1995:p.11). A mould for casting a *ge* from Houma, Shanxi features a bird in a similar style (Shanxi 1993:vol.1, p.95). Other comparable examples include a *ge* (Type II) and a *zun* (wine vessel, Type I) from Jinshengcun, Taiyuan (Shanxi 1996b:p.90 and p.108), as well as clay moulds from Houma (Shanxi 1993:vol.1, p.259, pl.144.7), which have in addition snakes similar to that of this dagger-axe (Shanxi 1993:vol.1, p.240, pl.131.4). This *ge* should be an example from the capital area of the Zhou State or of the Jin-type bronzes.

1.洛陽市文物工作隊《洛陽中州中路東周墓》，《文物》1995年第8期第11頁。

2.山西省考古研究所《侯馬鑄銅遺址》（上冊）第95頁，文物出版社1993年版。

3.山西省考古研究所、太原市文物管理委員會《太原晉國趙卿墓》第90、108頁，文物出版社1996年版。

4.同2第259頁、圖一四四·7。

5.同2第240頁、圖一三一·4。

58

交龍紋軎轄　春秋晚期（公元前6世紀上半葉–前476年）
甲：高8.3厘米　底徑8厘米　重615.9克
乙：高8.3厘米　底徑8厘米　重624.5克

　　一對。軎身整體作圓筒形，末端粗頂端細，頂端半封形成一圓孔，近頂處的軎身呈十二面體，其中一面鑄銘"吉用"，其下置一周凸棱，末端處兩側隆起，設大小兩個對穿的方孔，用於插轄，隆起部分的兩側亦有對穿的小圓孔，末端的圓口置一圈向外平折的寬緣。凸棱處飾有菱形卷雲紋，筒身裝飾交龍紋，龍身呈帶狀相互纏繞糾集，上面飾有鱗紋或短斜綫紋。上海博物館藏的鳥獸龍紋壺上有類似的紋飾[1]，在山西侯馬鑄銅遺址的陶範上也有發現[2]。兩側的方孔處飾獸首，只有獸目和上卷的獸角，突出部分作爲鼻、口，雖簡略但頗爲生動傳神。轄爲長條形，一端爲略呈長方形的帽。

　　軎轄是車器。軎套在車軸的兩端，用以加固軸頭。使用時，末端套接軸頭，轄插入方孔內，以防車輪的脫落。隆起處的四個小孔，是用以穿革帶和小木轄防止軎的移動，這是比較特殊的形制，河北邯鄲百家村M3：59[3]、河南汲縣山彪鎮M1：123[4]也是這種樣式。而末端置寬折緣的軎出現於春秋早期，這是車制構造上的一種改革，可以進一步穩固車轂、保護軸頭，春秋戰國以及漢代一直沿用。

A pair of wei xia
(axle cap and linch-pin)
with intertwined dragons

Late Spring and Autumn (first half of the 6th century – 476 BC)
A: height 8.3cm, diameter of base 8cm, weight 615.9g
B: height 8.3cm, diameter of base 8cm, weight 624.5g

This pair of *wei* has a dodecahedral top with a round hole in the center and an inscription 'Ji Yong'. Above the base are rectangular slots for the linch-pin. Lozenge shaped clouds decorate the ridges and for the rest of the body are intertwined dragons. Similar decorative designs can be found on a *hu* (wine vessel) with birds, animals and dragons in the collection of the Shanghai Museum (Zhongguo Qingtongqi 1995:pl.65), and on the clay moulds from the site of bronze foundry in Houma, Shanxi province (Shanxi 1996a). The rectangular slots appear as the mouths of animals with a protruding nose atop, and eyes and horns to the sides. The linch-pin (*xia*) has a rectangular cap at one end.

Wei and *xia* are used as cap and linch-pin for the axle of a carriage. To prevent wheels from falling off, the lower part of the *wei* is fasten on the axle by putting the *xia* through the retangular slots. To ensure that the *wei* is well fastened, leather straps or small wood linch-pins are put through the four small holes at the sides. This unusual design can be found in other examples (M3:59) from Baijiacun, Handan, Hebei Province (Hebei 1962:p.613), and (M1:123) from Shanbiaozhen, Jixian, Henan Province (Guo Baojun 1959:pl.28.3). *Wei* with such a wide and thick base appearing in the early Spring and Autumn period recorded an advancement in the mechanism of wheel-carriage and this kind of *wei* was used from the Spring and Autumn period to the Han dynasty.

1.中國青銅器全集編輯委員會《中國青銅器全集·8》圖版六五，文物出版社1995年版。
2.參見山西省考古研究所《侯馬陶範藝術》，美國普林斯敦大學出版社1996年版。
3.河北省文化局文物工作隊《河北邯鄲百家村戰國墓》，《考古》1962年第12期第613頁。
4.郭寶鈞《山彪鎮與琉璃閣》圖版二八：3，科學出版社1959年版。

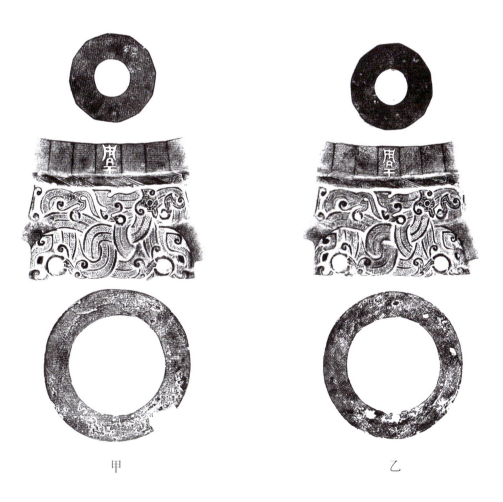

甲 乙

158

59

變形鳥紋鼎 戰國早期（公元前475年－前4世紀中葉）

高24.5厘米　口徑25厘米　腹深13.2厘米　腹徑28.9厘米　重4750克

　　造型爲扁球形。淺蓋，蓋設三個伏獸鈕，獸作回顧狀，體軀渾圓，蓋中間設兩頭獸首半環鈕，連接一圓環。器、蓋子母口。器斂口，淺腹圜底，附耳微曲，獸蹄足甚長，腹、足的連接處幾近腹中部。自蓋至腹部飾六周紋飾，皆以凸弦紋爲界。蓋面中間爲相背的對稱龍紋，綫條宛轉流暢似流雲紋；其餘紋飾均爲變形鳥紋間以卷雲紋，鳥紋兩兩相對，彎喙向上，頭部用圓目表現，體軀爲"S"形綫條；耳部的内、外側和耳廓亦飾相同的紋飾。足上部飾獸首紋。

　　此鼎的形制與曾侯乙墓出土的Ⅰ式蓋鼎[1]、湖北隨州擂鼓墩2號墓出土的Ⅰ式蓋鼎（M2：54）[2]、四川新都戰國墓出土的"邵鼎"相近[3]，蓋面中間的龍紋與包山2號楚墓出土直頸平肩壺（M2：179、M2：180）[4]上的紋飾接近，變形鳥紋與曾侯乙墓盤（C.148）[5]上的紋飾近似。因此，從造型和紋飾風格分析，這件鼎爲楚文化系統的青銅器。

Ding (food vessel) with stylized birds

Early Warring States (475 – mid 4th century BC)

Height 24.5cm, diameter of mouth 25cm, depth 13.2cm, diameter of belly 28.9cm, weight 4750g

In the shape of a compressed sphere, this tripod (cauldron) has a convex lid with three crouching animals along the rim and a ring knob at the center. The two handles and the three high legs are slighlty splayed. Raised rings divide the lid and body into six decorative bands. Back-to-back symmetric dragons mark the center of the lid while stylized birds and scrolling clouds appear in other bands. The birds, with S-shaped body and the head represented by a round eye, are all facing each other with beaks pointing upward. While the handles have the same decorative design, the legs are decorated with animal masks.

Three examples similar in form to this _ding_ are known, namely a lidded _ding_ (Type I) from the burial of Marquis Yi of Zeng (Hubei 1989:vol.1, p.196), a lidded _ding_ (M2:54, Type I) from burial No.2 in Leigudun, Suizhou, Hubei Province (Hubei 1985:p.22), and the Shao _ding_ from a Warring States burial in Xindu, Sichuan Province (Sichuan 1981:p.6). The dragon design on the lid is similar to that of a _hu_ (M: 179, 180) from the Chu burial No.2 at Baoshan (Hubei 1991:vol.1, p.105), and the bird design is similar to that of a _pan_ (C.148) from the burial of Marquis Yi of Zeng (Hubei 1989:vol.1, p.242). With all these similarities in style and decoration, this tripod can be identified as a bronze of Chu culture.

1.湖北省博物館《曾侯乙墓·上》第196頁，文物出版社1989年版。

2.湖北省博物館、隨州市博物館《湖北隨州擂鼓墩二號墓發掘簡報》，《文物》1985年第1期第22頁。

3.四川省博物館、新都縣文物管理所《四川新都戰國木椁墓》，《文物》1981年第6期第6頁。

4.湖北省荆沙鐵路考古隊《包山楚墓·上》第105頁，文物出版社1991年版。

5.同1第242頁。

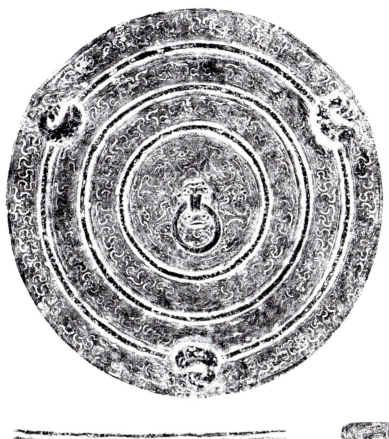

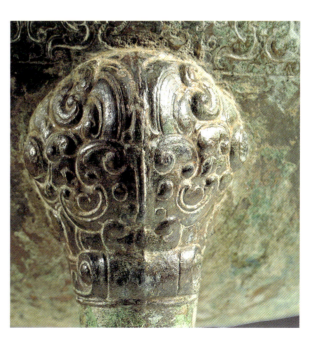

60

蟠龍紋鼎　戰國早期（公元前475年－前4世紀中葉）

高28.5厘米　口徑29.1厘米　腹深17.1厘米　腹徑32厘米　重7800克

形體似扁球形。斂口有蓋，蓋有三個環形紐，可却置，附耳，耳廓略弧曲，短獸蹄足。蓋鈕環形中間飾浮雕的小獸首，兩側爲雷紋組成的菱形紋。有一個值得注意的現象，在三個環鈕上的小獸首中，一個向外爲正面，兩個小獸首向内爲倒置，可能是作爲鼎的安置方向標誌。

蓋頂正中爲火紋，其外爲兩圈蟠龍紋，腹部中間以一周凸起的絢索紋爲界，亦飾上下兩層蟠龍紋。蟠龍紋的龍體粗壯，龍角呈曲尺狀聳起，體軀盤曲，蓋之内圈和腹部下端的龍紋尾部向一側伸展而相接，而蓋之外圈以及腹部上端的龍紋尾部向兩側展開並且相互纏繞。耳部的内、外側也飾有龍紋，上部爲相背的雙龍紋，兩龍首在中間，作回顧狀，體軀向兩面橫向展開；兩側的龍紋則呈"S"形。龍紋皆由寬綫條構成，内中填以細密的雷紋和幾何紋。耳部的外緣亦飾有絢紋，由兩平面的綫條相交構成，綫條内填以卷雲紋；而腹部的絢紋則由三條細綫紋構成的繩紋交錯相編而成，這是兩種結構不同的絢紋。足上部裝飾獸首。

此器和上海博物館所藏的一件龍紋鼎相似[1]，與山西金勝村大墓出土的M251:633鼎[2]、山西長子縣東周7號墓出土的Ⅰ式鼎[3]也比較類同，在山西侯馬銅鑄造遺址中出土有與此鼎的龍紋、絢紋等大致相同的陶範[4]，因此，從器形和紋飾看，這件鼎應屬晉系青銅器的遺物。

Ding (food vessel) with coiling dragons

Early Warring States (475 – mid 4th century BC)

Height 28.5cm, diameter of mouth 29.1cm, depth 17.1cm, diameter of belly 32cm, weight 7800g

Three short legs support the compressed spherical body with two splayed handles. The convex lid of this tripod has three upright rings with relief animal heads, one facing outward but the other two facing inward. This might give an indication of how the tripod should be palced.

Fire symbol marks the center of the lid, followed by two rings of dragons. The body is divided by a pattern of rope into two friezes of coiling dragons with angular horns. The dragons on the inner circle of the lid and the lower part of the belly extend their tails in one direction and twisted with others', while the dragons on the outer circle of the lid and the upper part of the belly have their tail extend separately in two directions. Various dragons appear on the two handles. All the dragons are formed by bands of _leiwen_ and geometric patterns. Patterns of rope on the handle and the belly are different. Animal masks can be found on the upper part of the legs.

This tripod is comparable to a _ding_ with dragons in the Shanghai Museum (Zhongguo Qingtongqi 1995:pl.22), and has similarities to a _ding_ (M251:633) from a burial in

1.中國青銅器全集編輯委員會《中國青銅器全集·8》第二二圖，文物出版社1995年版。

2.山西省考古研究所、太原市文物管理委員會《太原晉國趙卿墓》第21頁，文物出版社1996年版。

3.山西省考古研究所《山西長子縣東周墓》，《考古學報》1984年第4期第507頁。

4.參見山西省考古研究所《侯馬鑄銅遺址》（上）第205至223頁、第271頁，文物出版社1993年版。

Jinshengcun, Shanxi Province (Shanxi 1996b:p.21) and a ding
(Type I) from the Eastern Zhou burial No.7 in Zhangzi County,
Shanxi Province (Shanxi 1984:p.507). From the bronze foundry
sites in Houma, Shanxi, clay moulds with similar patterns of
dragons and plaited design have been discovered (Shanxi
1993:vol.1, pp.205-223 and p.271). This tripod can be identified
as an example of the Jin-type bronzes judging from the style and
decorative patterns.

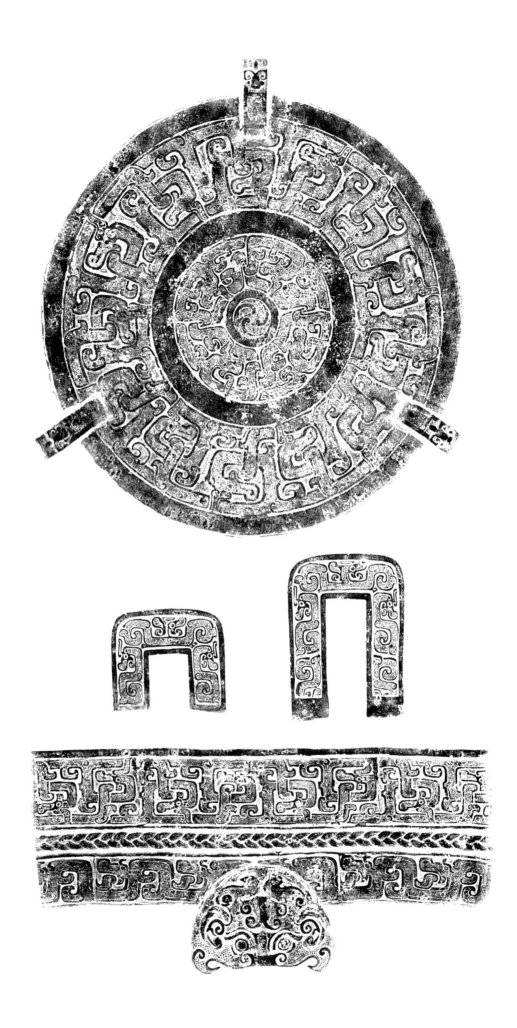

61

勾連雷紋敦　戰國早期（公元前475年－前4世紀中葉）

高15.9厘米　口徑16厘米　腹深7.2厘米　腹徑17.6厘米　重1577.5克

　　器、蓋形制基本相同，皆寬腹下收爲圓底，設有外侈的圈形捉手，腹部兩側各置一環耳。蓋的口沿處略收形成束頸，與器的子口相合，這是此類敦造型上的一個特徵。捉手内底中間飾六瓣葉形紋，其外爲各式雲雷紋，外圈鱗紋間飾幾何紋，捉手的内壁飾一周三角幾何紋。環耳飾有陰綫的幾何雲紋。器、蓋均裝飾勾連雷紋，由斜的山字形綫條相互連接構成，並以細密的小圓粒紋填充空隙。陝西省博物館藏亦藏有一件勾連雷紋敦，高17厘米，形制和紋飾與此器基本相同[1]。

　　這件器物的形制與河南陝縣戰國早期墓出土敦（M2040:274）相似[2]，也近於長治分水嶺戰國早期墓出土敦（M26:13）[3]，具有三晉青銅器風格。敦是盛放飯食的器具，出現在春秋中期，春秋晚期和戰國時期比較流行。其基本形制有兩種，一種是蓋、器對稱，具有兩耳三足，少量爲圈足，上述三件敦屬於圈足類；另一種爲上下不對稱，形制有較大的差別。

　　勾連雷紋，自商晚期至戰國青銅器上均有裝飾，通行時間很長，結構基本相似，實則不盡相同。上海博物館所藏的春成侯盉、長子盉上也裝飾了同樣結構的勾連雷紋。近年來有學者認爲，這兩件盉之銘文中的"龘"字，即指盉腹上的勾連雷紋，爲當時的一種裝飾在絲織品、竹製品、玉石製品、青銅器上的花紋，所以也可以稱爲"龘紋"[4]。

1.陝西歷史博物館《尋覓散落的瑰寶》第22頁，三秦出版社2001年版。

2.中國社會科學院考古研究所《陝縣東周秦漢墓》第56頁，科學出版社1994年版。

3.山西省文物管理委員會、山西省考古研究所《山西長治分水嶺戰國墓第二次發掘》，《考古》1964年第3期第126頁。

4.唐友波《春成侯盉與長子盉綜合研究》，《上海博物館集刊》第八期第151頁，上海書畫出版社2000年版。

Dui (food vessel) with pattern of connecting thunder

Early Warring States (475 – mid 4th century BC)
Height 15.9cm, diameter of mouth 16cm, depth 7.2cm, diameter of belly 17.6cm, weight 1577.5g

The two halves of this round vessel are in the same shape. The bowl stands on a foot-ring while the cover has a round splayed handle. As a feature of the *dui* vessel, the rim of the cover is slightly contracted to fit the bowl. Six-petalled leaves appear at the centre of the round handle, surrounded by *leiwen* patterns and a circle of scales and geometric patterns. The inside wall of the handle is decorated with a circle of triangles. The four ring lugs at the sides have engraved geometric clouds. The cover and the bowl have pattern of connecting thunder (made up of "凵"-shaped lines) against a ring-matted ground. In the Shaanxi History Museum is a *dui* (17cm in height) with same form and decorative patterns (Shaanxi 2001:p.22).

Like a *dui* (M2040:274) from an early Warring States burial in Shanxian, Henan Province (Zhongguo 1994b:p.56), and another one (M26:13) from an early Warring States burial in Fenshuiling, Changzhi (Shanxi 1964:p.126), this present example has the characteristics of the three States of the former Jin territory. *Dui* as a container for food and rice appeared in the mid Spring and Autumn period, and became popular in the late Spring and Autumn to the Warring States period. Two types of *dui* are known: one has symmetry between the cover and the bowl, two handles and three legs, sometimes a foot-ring instead; the other type with no symmetry includes a variety of forms.

Patterns of connecting thunder with variations were popular for the bronzes from the late Shang to the Warring States period. Two *he* in the Shanghai Museum have thunder pattern similar to this piece. Certain scholars think that the character '*fu*' inscribed on the two *he* refers to this thunder pattern, which is a design commonly seen on silk, bamboo handiwork, jades, and bronzes, and it well be named the *fu* pattern (Tang Youbo 2000:p.151).

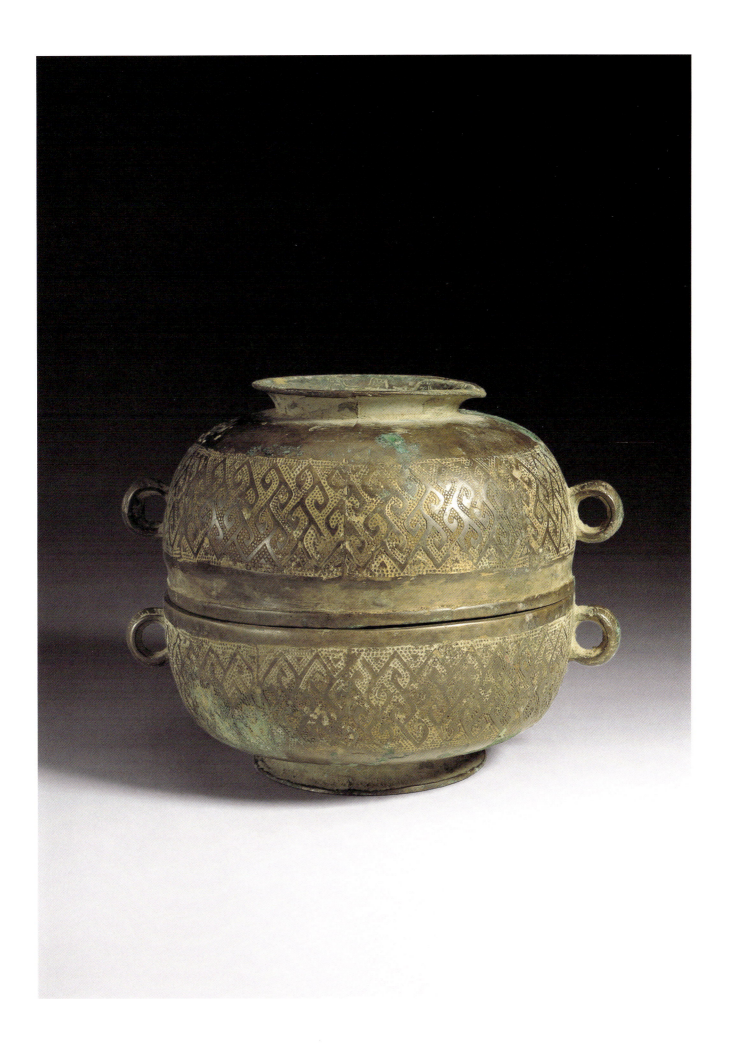

62

宴射刻紋畫像匜

戰國早期（公元前475年－前4世紀中葉）

高11.9厘米　流至口長22厘米　腹深6.8厘米　重330克

　　橢圓體，器壁極薄。前有斜伸的長流，後有寬環鈕，平底，環鈕與器壁用鉚接方法相連。器壁內淺刻紋飾。流口刻有三魚紋，中間一條向外，兩邊向內各一條；器壁近流口處有七組水波紋。其下的弧形半圈內設有一案，案上置二壺，一壺內放有長柄勺，案之一旁頭戴三叉冠者一手持觚一手拿勺；正準備酓酒，其身後一人雙手持豆，兩人相對而坐，中間放一豆，其中一人持觚而飲，另一旁戴長冠者一手持觚一手欲取酒勺，其身後兩人相對躬身，其中一人持觚，是爲貴族宴享圖。宴享圖兩側的上方爲排列齊整的灌木小樹。一側的內壁爲人物、樹木，其中一人手足並用攀爬大樹，另一側的兩棵大樹上各停一鶴，樹下又有一鶴低頭覓食，樹前有一人對準樹上之鶴正欲張弓放箭。內壁的後端爲一塊織物繫在兩根斜撐的竿子上，中央有同心圓圈，這是射禮所用的射布，即箭靶，稱爲"侯"。《儀禮·鄉射禮》："乃張侯下網。"鄭玄注："侯，謂所射布也。""侯"一旁杆上的旒迎風飄揚，另一旁有飛鶴展翅翱翔。內壁的近底處刻有一圈三角幾何紋。內底刻有相互纏繞的蛇紋，頭近三角形，體軀肥碩。

　　這件匜的紋飾綫條是用銳利的鋒刃鏨刻的，細察之，綫條並不連貫，由一刀一段的契形短綫構成，細如毫髮，刻工十分嫻熟。在畫面的安排上十分注重故事情節的展開，給人以有條不紊之感；所刻的人物、禽鳥也是神態生動、栩栩如生；而在流口處刻游動的魚，與水流相應，在器底刻纏繞呈圓形的蛇紋，注重了紋飾與功用和器形的協調。畫像刻紋出現於春秋晚期，流行於戰國早中期，以繪畫的形式表現了豐富多彩的社會生活情景，它擺脫了以往青銅器裝飾中規律化的對稱圖案，使得構圖自由，綫條流暢，拓展了青銅器裝飾的內容和方法。

　　與此器有相近紋飾者見於湖南長沙楚墓[1]、河南陝縣後川戰國墓[2]、山西潞城潞河戰國墓[3]、江蘇鎮江諫壁王家山[4]所出之匜，研究表明，這些器物的年代多爲戰國早期[5]。

Yi (water vessel) with engraved figures

Early Warring States (475 – mid 4th century BC)

Height 11.9cm, length 22cm, depth 6.8cm, weight 330g

The *yi* has an ovoid bowl with a long spout, a ring handle and a flat bottom. The wall of the vessel is very thin, and the handle is jointed together with rivets. Various engraved patterns decorate the interior of the vessel. Three fish, one in the middle facing outward and the other two facing inward, are seen at the spout, followed by seven groups of wave pattern and a banquet scene on the bowl. Someone is drinking wine from a *gu* and some people are using ladles to fill their *gu* with wine. In the groves are people climbing a tree and aiming his bow at the cranes on the trees. A *hou*, a cloth target with concentric circles, is depicted hanging between two poles. On the bottom are intertwined serpentines encircled within a ring of triangles.

1.湖南省博物館等《長沙楚墓》（上）第159頁，文物出版社2000年版。

2.中國社會科學院考古研究所《陝縣東周秦漢墓》第64頁，科學出版社1994年版。

3.山西省考古研究所、山西省晉東南地區文化局《山西省潞城縣潞河戰國墓》，《文物》1986年第1期第1頁。

4.鎮江博物館《江蘇鎮江諫壁王家山東周墓》，《文物》1987年第12期第25頁。

5.周亞《丹徒諫壁王家山東周墓部份青銅器的時代及其他》，《上海博物館集刊》第六期第164頁，上海古籍出版社1992年版。

The patterns on the vessel are engraved with sharp tools in broken lines formed by fine and short cuts. All the figures and animals are vividly depicted and perfectly arranged, for instance, the fish and the serpentine decorating the spout and the round bottom respectively. Bronzes engraved with figures appeared in the late Spring and Autumn period, and became popular in the early to mid Warring States period. With the addition of scenes of daily lives to the previous patterned designs, the decoration of bronzes turned a new page.

Examples with similar decorative themes are available from a Chu burial in Changsha, Hunan Province (Hunan 2000:vol.1,p.159), a Warring States burial in Houchuan, Shanxian, Henan Province (Zhongguo 1994b:p.64), a Warring States burial in Luhe, Lucheng, Shanxi Province (Shanxi 1986:p.1), and also from Wangjiahan in Jianbi, Zhenjiang, Jiangsu Province (Zhenjiang 1987:p.25). These *yi* vessels are all dated to the early Warring States period (Zhou Ya 1992:p.164).

170

63

變形鳥紋鼎

戰國早期（公元前475年－前4世紀中葉）

高23.1厘米　口徑19.9厘米　腹深13.4厘米　腹徑22.9厘米　重3510克

　　器、蓋相合，造型呈扁圓體。蓋設四個牛形鈕，牛同向環列而臥，頭部抬起，雙角後聳，圓目，雙耳竪起，體軀側臥，前、後腿曲伸。口沿兩側有附耳，其上端侈張幾近平面。腹底弧曲較緩，下接三蹄足。

　　蓋頂中心飾火紋，其外的寬弦紋圈内爲三條俯視狀的龍紋，龍身由小圓珠組成，背部有一條凸脊，蜿蜒潜行，體軀兩側各設有兩對龍爪，在紋飾的空隙處飾有雷紋。蓋面外側、器腹部的上部和下部各裝飾三圈變形鳥紋，這種鳥紋比較特殊，圓眼，彎喙，整體近似橢方形，連續排列，頗爲華麗。耳部的内外側飾有龍紋。蹄足上部裝飾獸首紋。

　　這件鼎與河北平山縣戰國中山國靈壽城6號墓出土的五件羞鼎近似[1]，特別是變形鳥紋更爲相近，而6號墓所出的提梁盉也裝飾了這種紋飾[2]，這類變形鳥紋的圖案在侯馬出土陶範上亦有[3]。這件鼎的蓋鈕，其風格特徵與山西太原金勝村晉國大墓出土升鼎蓋鈕以及侯馬鑄銅遺址出土的牛紋範相似[4]，而蓋面中間的龍紋，又與河北懷來北辛堡戰國燕國墓地出土的交龍紋壺（M1:87）蓋面的紋飾幾乎相同[5]。中山國爲北方游牧民族白狄建立的諸侯國，春秋時期稱爲鮮虞，戰國時期以"中山"爲名。由於中山國處在燕、三晉等大國之間，深受中原華夏民族的影響。這些集周邊文化於一體的現象，構成了中山國銅器的特色。

Ding (food vessel) with stylized birds

Early Warring States (475 – mid 4th century BC)

Height 23.1cm, diameter of mouth 19.9cm, depth 13.4cm, diameter of belly 22.9cm, weight 3510g

This *ding*, in the shape of a compressed sphere with three hoof-shaped legs, has a convex lid with four ox knobs. The handles are strongly bent.

Fire pattern marks the centre of the lid, which has three dragons in a raised ring. Stylized birds appear outside the ring, and also in the upper and lower parts of the belly. These birds with round eyes and hook beaks are very special. In an ovoid rectangular shape, they are arranged continuously and look rather magnificent. The handles are decorated with dragons, and the legs with animal masks.

This tripod is similar to the five Xiu *ding* from a Warrting States burial (M6) in the Lingshou fortress of the Zhongshan State in Pingshan County, Hebei Province, especially in the stylized birds (Hebei 2005:p.139). Besides, a *he* (water vessel) with a handle from the same burial has the same kind of stylized birds (Hebei 2005:p.143), which are also found on clay moulds from Houma (Shanxi 1993:vol.1, pl.157.3). Similar ox-shaped

---

1.河北省文物研究所《戰國中山國靈壽城》第139頁，文物出版社2005年版。

2.同上第143頁。

3.山西省考古研究所《侯馬鑄銅遺址》（上）圖157·3，文物出版社1993年。

4.山西省考古研究所、太原市文物管理委員會《太原晉國趙卿墓》第21頁，文物出版社1996年版；山西省考古研究所《侯馬鑄銅遺址》（上）第256頁，文物出版社1993年版。

5.河北省文化局文物工作隊《河北懷來北辛堡戰國墓》，《考古》1965年第5期第231頁；中國青銅器全集編輯委員會《中國青銅器全集·9》第一一七圖，文物出版社1997年版。

knobs are known on the lid of the Sheng tripod from the
Jin grave in Jinshengcun, Taiyuan, Shanxi Province, and
in clay moulds with oxen from the bronze foundry site of
Houma (Shanxi 1996b:p.21; Shanxi 1993:vol.1, p.256).
Furthermore, the dragons are almost identical to that of the
lid of a *hu* with intertwined dragons (M1:87) from a Yan
State burial at Beixinbao, Huailai, Hebei Province (Hebei
1965:p.231; Zhongguo Qingtongqi 1997:pl.117). The
Zhongshan State was established by Baidi, a nomadic tribe
in northern China. Formerly known as the Xianyu State in
the Spring and Autumn period, it changed to 'Zhongshan'
during the Warring States period. Geographically it was
the neighbour of the Yan State and the three States of the
former Jin, hence, it was deeply influenced by Chinese in
the central plain (*Zhongyuan*) and Zhongshan bronzes were
eclectic in style.

64

絢紋鼎

戰國早期（公元前475年－前4世紀中葉）

高14.1厘米　口徑12.6厘米　腹深9.6厘米　腹徑15.2厘米　重997.5克

　　隆蓋、器口內斂，器、蓋子母口。蓋設三個小鳥形鈕，頭向外等分環列，鳥作臥姿，圓眼，嘴部扁平，羽翅清晰可辨，造型生動。器腹扁圓，下接矮蹄足。腹部兩側爲鋪首銜環耳。蓋與器相合使整體造型渾然一體。蓋面飾內外兩圈絢紋，器腹上下各飾一道絢紋，皆由兩條波綫交錯而成；器腹中間飾一周連續的貝紋。

　　絢紋鼎的造型特徵與山西太原金勝村、山西長子縣、洛陽西宮戰國墓出土的扁圓體矮足鼎相同[1]，洛陽西宮出土者自銘爲“軌”，爲研究這類器物的功用提供了重要資料。水鳥形蓋鈕見於陝縣後川戰國鼎（M2149:1）[2]，亦見於山西長子戰國墓鼎（M1:3）[3]，三者造型極爲相似，而山西侯馬鑄銅遺址則出土有這種鼎鈕的陶範[4]。絢紋和貝紋同於上海博物館所藏的鳥獸龍紋壺圈足上的紋飾[5]，侯馬鑄銅遺址出土的陶範上也有發現[6]。

　　從這件鼎的形制、蓋鈕、所飾的紋飾來看，其年代爲戰國早期，其鑄造地應當爲山西侯馬鑄銅作坊。

Ding (food vessel) with rope pattern

Early Warring States (475–mid 4th century BC)

Height 14.1cm, diameter of mouth 12.6cm, depth 9.6cm, diameter of belly 15.2cm, weight 997.5g

The short legs of this *ding* tripod fuse with the body's rounded contours. The vessel with two mask-and-ring handles at opposite sides is covered with a convex lid. Three crouching birds with round eyes, flat beaks and feathered wings are set at equidistance on the lid. Two rings of rope pattern decorate the lid, and another two on the belly enclosing continuous cowries.

This tripod is comparable in style to *ding* tripods unearthed from Warring States burials in Jinshengcun, Taiyuan, Shanxi Province, in Zhangzi County, Shanxi Province, and at Xigong, Luoyang (Shanxi 1996b:pls.18 and 19; Shanxi 1984:pl.20.5; Du Naisong 1964:p47). The one from Xigong is labeled a '*gui*' in the inscription, providing important information to the study of its function. Lids with similar bird knobs are known, first, a tripod (M2149:1) of the Warring States period from Houchuan, Shanxian (Zhongguo 1994b:p.55), and second, a tripod (M1:3) from a Warring States burial in Zhangzi, Shanxi Province (Shanxi 1984:p.519). Clay moulds for this kind of knobs have been found in the bronze foundry site of Houma (Shanxi 1993:vol.1, p.256). The patterns of rope and cowry are the same as that of the foot-ring of a *hu* with birds, dragons and animals in the Shanghai Museum (Zhongguo Qingtongqi 1995:pl.65). Once again, clay moulds from the Houma foundry site have also these patterns (Shanxi 1993:vol.1, pp.261-262, 271-272).

---

1. 山西省考古研究所、太原市文物管理委員會《太原晉國趙卿墓》圖版18、19，文物出版社1996年版；山西省考古研究所《山西長子縣東周墓》，《考古學報》1984年第4期圖版二十·5；杜迺松《記洛陽西宮出土的幾件銅器》，《文物》1964年第11期第47頁。
2. 中國社會科學院考古研究所《陝縣東周秦漢墓》第55頁，科學出版社1994年版。
3. 山西省考古研究所《山西長子縣東周墓》，《考古學報》1984年第4期第519頁。
4. 山西省考古研究所《侯馬鑄銅遺址》（上）第256頁，文物出版社1993年版。
5. 中國青銅器全集編輯委員會《中國青銅器全集·8》第六五圖，文物出版社1995年版。
6. 山西省考古研究所《侯馬鑄銅遺址》（上）第261、262、271、272頁，文物出版社1993年版。

Judging from the shape and decoration as well as the knobs of the lid, this tripod can be dated to the early Warring States period, and was probably made in the bronze foundry of Houma, Shanxi Province.

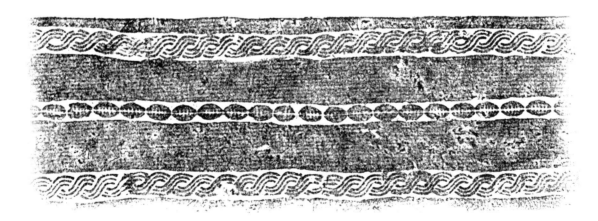

177

65

交龍紋筒形器

戰國中晚期（公元前4世紀中葉－前221年）

高22.7厘米　口徑9厘米　腹深19.8厘米　腹徑8.2厘米　重673.8克

　　淺弧蓋，設三環鈕，蓋、器子母口，器體作口大底小的筒形，器壁略弧，矮圈足。蓋面呈瓦楞狀，腹部飾三周交龍紋帶，龍爲S形，兩端皆有龍首，體軀相互交連。此器的形制比較少見，山東諸城臧家莊發現的青銅器中兩件器[1]，與之比較近同，但腹部兩側有環耳，《西清古鑒》卷21也著錄過相似的器物，諸城臧家莊青銅器屬於齊國，其年代約爲戰國中期偏晚。器腹所飾的交龍紋，見於甘肅平涼廟莊戰國墓出土銅鼎（M6:1）[2]、陝西咸陽塔兒坡出土中郾鼎與平鼎[3]，從墓葬和同出青銅器分析年代爲戰國中晚期。據形制、銘文、紋飾，這些鼎雖出於秦墓，但皆爲三晉、東周等地的器物，被秦人掠奪而來[4]，這件交龍紋筒形器亦當出自這些地區，其年代爲戰國中晚期。

Beaker with intertwined dragons

Mid to late Warring States (mid 4th century – 221 BC)
Height 22.7cm, diameter of mouth 9cm, depth 19.8cm, diameter of belly 8.2cm, weight 673.8g

A tall, tumbler-like vessel with a tapering body and a low foot-ring, and its convex lid has three rings. Three bands of intertwined S-shape dragons with double heads decorate the body. Vessels in such an unusual shape are rarely known. Two similar examples with two additional ring handles on the body have been discovered from Zangjiazhuang in Zhucheng, Shandong Province (Qi Wentao 1972:p.14), and in *Xiqing gujian* (juan 21) are descriptions of.comparable vessels. The vessels from Shandong belong to the Qi State of the mid Warring States period. The intertwined dragons on this present example are similar to that of a *ding* from a Warring States burial (M6:1) at Miaozhuang, Pingliang, Gansu Province (Gansu 1982:p.27), and two *ding* from the burials of the mid to late Warring States period at Ta'erpo, Xianyang, Shaanxi Province (Xianyang 1975:p.69). Although these *ding* were excavated from the burials of the Qin State, they were apparently made in the areas of the Jin or the Eastern Zhou but were taken away by the Qin raiders (Zhu Fenghan 1995:ch.13, sec.3, no.5). This beaker was probably made also in the areas of the Jin or the Eastern Zhou and can be dated to the mid to late Warring States period.

1.齊文濤《概述近年來山東出土的商周青銅器》，《文物》1972年底5期第14頁。

2.甘肅省博物館、魏懷珩《甘肅平涼廟莊的兩座戰國墓》，《考古與文物》1982年第5期第27頁。

3.咸陽市博物館《陝西咸陽塔兒坡出土的銅器》，《文物》1975年第6期第69頁。

4.參見朱鳳瀚《古代中國青銅器》第十三章第三節·五，南開大學出版社1995年版。

179

66

五 套 筒 形 器　戰國中晚期（公元前4世紀中葉－前221年）

最大高14.8厘米　口徑5.6厘米　腹深12.7厘米　最小高10.3厘米　口徑4.8厘米　腹深9.7厘米

總重646.2克

　　器爲五件套，形制相同，大小漸次遞減，均素面無紋。造型與交龍紋筒形器相同，最大的一件有瓦楞紋蓋，蓋面中心有一個小突刺。這五件套裝後非常密縫，風格精巧別致，顯示了出色的鑄作技術。河北滿城漢墓所出的鎏金菱形紋杯（M1:4273）[1]，具有相近的造型，只是腹壁較直，同墓所出九件鉢形器，也可套裝[2]，該墓的墓主爲西漢中山靖王劉勝。這説明此種樣式的筒形器一直沿用至西漢，而器物套裝的特徵也被傳襲。

Five-piece set of beakers

Mid to late Warring States (mid 4th century – 221 BC)

The biggest one: height 14.8cm, diameter of mouth 5.6cm, depth 12.7cm

The smallest one: height 10.3cm, diameter of mouth 4.8cm, depth 9.7cm

Overall weight 646.2g

These five plain cylindrical vessels form a nesting set. The form is the same as the previous example. The lid of the biggest one has coiled ridges and a small loop at the center. The five pieces are perfectly fit inside each other. From the Western Han burial of Liu Sheng, the Prince of Zhongshan Principality in Mancheng, Hebei Province (Zhongguo 1980c:p.78) is a gilt cylinder vessel with lozenge pattern (M1:4273), which is similar in shape to the present examples though the body is comparatively straight. From the same burial is a nest of nine bowls (Zhongguo 1980c:p.60). It shows that beaker sets of this kind as well as nests of bronzes continued to be popular even in the Western Han period.

1.中國社會科學院考古研究所、河北省文物管理處《滿城漢墓發掘報告》第78頁，文物出版社1980年版。

2.同上第60頁。

67

商 鞅 鈹

戰國中晚期（公元前4世紀中葉－前221年）
長52.1厘米　寬4.4厘米　重666.2克

鈹身中綫起脊，莖作扁條狀，刃部比較鋒利。近莖處中脊兩側的從部刻有銘文兩行16字：

十六年大良造庶長

鞅之造畢湍侯之鑄。

銘文中"十六年"爲秦孝公十六年（公元前346），"鞅"即商鞅。大良造、庶長皆爲爵位。據《史記·秦本紀》，秦孝公六年"乃拜鞅爲左庶長"，"十年，衛鞅爲大良造"。左庶長是秦爵位的第十二級，大良造是秦爵位的第十六級，《漢書·百官公卿表》又稱"大上造"，兩種爵位均屬於高等級的爵位[1]。傳世和出土商鞅監造的兵器尚有數件，如：

1.十三年大良造鞅戟[2]

2.十六年大良造鞅殳鐓[3]

3.十九年大良造鞅殳鐓[4]

4.十□年大良造鞅殳鐓[5]

這些兵器的銘文明確記録了三點：首先是鑄造時間即紀年；其次是以中央掌權者商鞅爲監造，表明鑄造權屬於中央政府；再者是鑄造地和製造者的名字。十六年大良造鞅鈹銘文也具備了這三個特點。

Pi (spear-like sword) made with supervision of Shang Yang

Mid to late Warring States (mid 4th century – 221 BC)
Length 52.1cm, width 4.4cm, weight 666.2g

This sword with a flat hilt and sharp blade edges has a ridge in the middle of the blade. On the two sides of the blade is a two-column sixteen-character inscription, reading '*Shiliunian Daliangzao Shuzhang, Yang zhizao Bichuan Hou zhizhu* (In the sixteenth year Daliangzao Shuzhang Yang supervised this production for Marquis of Bi Chuan)'. It was the sixteenth year of the reign of Duke Xiao of Qin. Yang refers to Shang Yang. Daliangzao and Shuzhang both are titles of dukedom. It is recorded in *Shiji (Records of the Grand Historian)* that Shang Yang was conferred Left Shuzhang (12th rank) in the sixth year of the Duke Xiao reign, and the Daliangzao (16th rank) in the tenth year. Both were high rank dukedom (Yang Kuan 1998:p.253). Marquis of Bichuan is the chief of Bichuan, but no records can be found in historical texts.

Four other weapons with inscription of Shang Yang are known among heirloom pieces and excavated artifacts:

1.參閱楊寬《戰國史（增訂本）》第253頁，上海人民出版社1998年版。

2.馬承源《商周青銅器銘文選》（第二冊）第922器，文物出版社1987年版。現藏上海博物館。

3.中國社會科學院考古研究所《殷周金文集成》第十八冊11911，中華書局1994年版。現藏故宮博物院。

4.咸陽市文物考古研究所《咸陽石油鋼管鋼繩廠秦墓清理簡報》圖4，《考古與文物》1996年第5期。

5.于省吾《雙劍誃古器物圖録》上卷四十九。現藏中國國家博物館。

1 *Ji, Shisannian Daliangzao Yang* (In the thirteenth year supervised by Daliangzao Yang) (Now in the collection of the Shanghai Museum, see Ma Chengyuan 1987:vol.2, pl.922)

2 *Shudun, Shiliunian Daliangzao Yang* (In the sixteenth year supervised by Daliangzao Yang) (Now in the collection of the Palace Museum, Beijing, see Zhongguo 1994a:fig.11911)

3 *Shudun, Shijiunian Daliangzao Yang* (In the nineteenth year supervised by Daliangzao Yang) (Xianyang 1996:fig.4)

4 *Shudun, Shi* ☐ *nian Daliangzao Yang* (In the xx [indecipherable] year supervised by Daliangzao Yang) (Now in the collection of Chinese National Museum, Beijing, see Yu Xingwu 1940:vol.1, pl.49)

The inscriptions on these weapons have three features: first, recording the date of production; second, identifying the supervisor Shang Yang, which indicates that they were made for the central government; and third, telling where these weapons were made and who made them. The inscription of the present sword includes all such information; however, it mentions in addition the title of the local chief. Bi was a feudal state given by King Wen of Zhou to his son Duke Gao of Bi, located to the northwest of Chang'an County. Further research is required to find out whether 'Bichuan' was related to 'Bi'.

The four afore-metioned weapons and the Shang Yang *Fang Sheng* (bronze rectangular capacity measure supervised by Shang Yang) (Now in the collection of the Shanghai Museum, see Ma Chengyuan 1987:vol.2, pl.923) are known as the 'Five Objects of Shang Yang'. With this sword here, we have now 'Six Objects'.

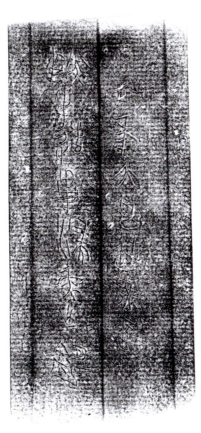
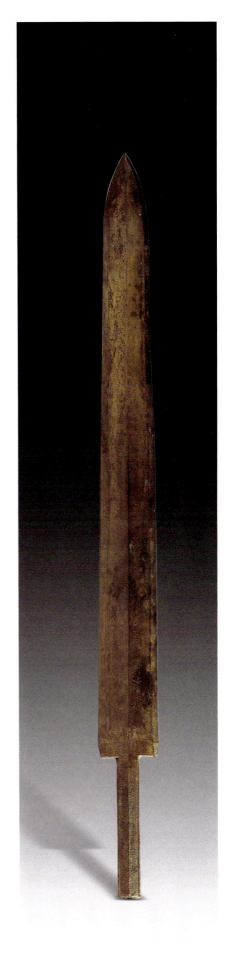

68

戈

戰國中晚期（公元前4世紀中葉－前221年）

長31.4厘米　寬26.8厘米　闌長20.3厘米　內長12.3厘米　重579.9克

　　援上揚，中脊綫秀挺，外側略呈弧形，援下刃處、胡中部內側各有一個鋒利的棘突形成曲胡刃，前鋒尖銳，近闌處設四狹長方穿，上端爲三角形的尖角，長內上揚，有三角形斜長穿。除援、胡之外，胡的下端，內的三面皆設刃，刃皆有折綫，鋒利異常。另外，大部戈體還保持銅質本色，從中可以觀察到當時精良的鑄作技術。顯然，此戈爲一件實用兵器，具有極大的殺傷力。

　　戈的援的上刃和內的上緣不平行，援身上揚甚大，這種樣式出現在春秋時期，到戰國早期已經成爲戈的主流，戰國墓中出土戈很大部分爲此類[1]。當然，如此戈之援、內形成明顯的角度，也是發展到了極致，這是頗爲少見的現象。

Ge (dagger-axe)

Mid to late Warring States (mid 4th century – 221 BC)

Length 31.4cm, width 26.8cm, length of banister 20.3cm, length of tang 12.3cm, weight 579.9g

This dagger-axe has an upward tilted blade with a sharp ridge in the middle. The blade is connected to the dewlap by a crescent terminated in projections. Four narrow apertures with triangle tops are set on the banister. The long tang also bears a triangle long aperture. The blade, *yuan*, outer and lower part of dewlap, and the tang are all with very sharp cutting edges. Furthermore, most of the dagger-axe still preserves the original bronze color, testifying to the high standard in the casting technique of the time. Obviously this *ge* was a very practical lethal weapon.

The style of this *ge* with unparallel upper blade and upper tang appeared during the Spring and Autumn period, and had became the main style from the early Warring States period. Most of the *ge* from Warring States burials belong to this style (Li Jianmin & Wu Jia'an 1991:p.104). However, such a large angle between the blade and the tang in this *ge* is rarely found.

1.參見李健民、吳家安《中國古代青銅戈》，《考古學集刊》第7期第104頁、科學出版社1991年版。

69

兩詔橢升

秦（公元前221年－前206年）

高6.2厘米　長21.9厘米　腹深5.8厘米　重997克

　　量器。橢圓形，腹較深，一端有方形中空的短銎柄。外壁一側刻秦始皇二十六年（公元前221）詔書：

廿六年皇帝

盡并兼天下

諸侯黔首大

安立號爲皇

帝乃詔丞相

狀綰灋度量

則不壹歉疑

者皆明壹之。

　　另一側刻秦二世元年（公元前209）詔書：

元年皇帝詔

丞相斯去疾

灋度量盡始

皇帝爲之皆

有刻辭焉今

襲號而刻辭

不稱始皇帝

其于久遠殹

如後嗣爲之

者不稱成功

盛德刻此

詔故刻左使毋疑。

　　戰國時期，各國的度量衡制度相當混亂，但秦國在商鞅第二次變法（公元前350）之後，就長期實行統一的度量衡政策，度量衡器比較一致。統一六國後，秦始皇以秦制爲基礎，在始皇二十六年下詔統一全國度量衡，這道詔書多銘刻在國家法定的度量衡的標準器和日用器上，這件器物即爲其中的一件。此器另一側的秦二世詔書，強調統一度量衡是秦始皇的功績，並將統一度量衡的法令繼續推行下去。

　　上海博物館也藏有一件兩詔橢升，據實測其容積爲654毫升[1]，而這件橢升的容積經用小米測量爲642毫升，兩者相差不大。

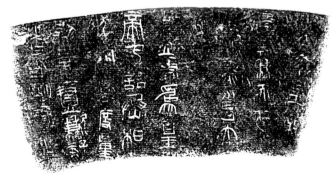

1.馬承源《商鞅方升和戰國量制》，《文物》1972年第6期第17頁。

Tuo sheng (ovoid capacity measure) with two imperial edicts

Qin (221 – 206 BC)

Height 6.2cm, length 21.9cm, depth 5.8cm, weight 997g

This object was originally used as a standard for measuring capacity. With ovoid shape and deep belly, it has a hollow square handle. One side of the vessel inscribed the edict from the First Emperor in the 26th year of his reign (221 BC), which reads, 'In the 26th year, the emperor united all feudal states, and people have peace. He proclaimed himself as Emperor. The prime minister was ordered to investigate the different standards in measurements, and convert them into this new standard.' The edict from Qin Ershi, son of the First Emperor, in the first year of his reign (209 BC) was inscribed on the other side of the vessel. It reads, 'This edict was made in the first year. The prime minister made the standard measurements, which were ordered by the First Emperor and inscriptions were marked on those vessels. Now, the new emperor has ascended to the throne. If in the inscription the First Emperor was not mentioned, after some time later generations will forget the great deeds of the First Emperor. Hence this edict is inscribed besides the first one so as to record the truth.'

During the Warring States period, different measuring systems and standards were used at the different states, causing great confusion. After the second reform of Shang Yang (in 350 BC), a unified measurement standard was used in the Qin State. Thus, the First Emperor of Qin issued the above edict to enforce a standard measurement system for all over the country in the 26th year of his reign, when he united all the six Warring States. This edict was usually inscribed on the standard measures or daily utensils. This *sheng* is one of such standard measures, but it also bears another edict from the second emperor of Qin to reiterate this great deed of his father and let this edict to last forever.

Another *tuo sheng* with two edicts in the collection of the Shanghai Museum has a capacity of 654 ml (Ma Chengyuan 1972:p.17). The capacity of this piece (measured with rice), 642 ml, is similar.

70

錯金銀鳥獸紋弩機

西漢（公元前206年－公元8年）
長11.2厘米　重568.1克

　　弩機均施以錯金銀裝飾。望山的一面爲孔雀紋和玄武，另一面爲雀鳥、仙鶴、獵豹，獵豹的項圈清晰可辨，側面爲龍紋；雙牙飾奔鹿、鳥紋；樞軸飾鳥紋。郭臺的後部爲白虎嚙野猪，白虎昂首張口，形體似弓，張力十足，野猪肥碩笨拙，白虎的後面，一隻長角鹿落荒而逃，另外還有飛禽、小獸散間其中，郭臺的前部則爲兩組對稱的奔鹿圖。最精彩的是箭槽中的圖案：一枝金色利箭脱弦而出，前方三隻大雁張開雙翅，奮力飛翔，企圖逃離險境，大雁的神態刻劃得栩栩如生。這件弩機上的紋飾與江蘇泗水王陵出土弩機相似[1]。

　　弩是用機械力射箭的弓，是由弓發展而成的一種遠程射殺傷性武器。弩由銅製弩機、木臂、弓三部分組成。弩的關鍵部件是弩機，弩機安裝在木臂的後部，其機件有郭、望山（瞄准器）、牙、懸刀（扳機）、機塞，和兩個將各部位組合爲整體的樞軸。張弦裝箭時，手拉望山，牙上升，機塞被帶起，其下齒鉗在懸刀刻口内，這樣，就可以用牙扣住弓弦，將箭置於弩臂上方的箭槽内，使箭栝頂在兩牙之間的弦上，通過望山瞄準目標往後扳動懸刀，牙下縮，箭即隨弦的回彈而射出。

　　考古發掘中所見年代較早的銅弩機，出土於山東曲阜魯故城的墓葬中的3號墓、52號墓中[2]，墓葬的年代約爲戰國早期，但尚無銅郭，弩機是裝在木臂掏空形成的郭内。漢代弩機使用廣泛，郭皆爲銅製，使弩能够承載更大的拉力，望山的内側或出現刻度用於瞄準，顯然，戰鬥性能更爲强大。

Nu (crossbow) inlaid with gold and silver patterns of birds and animals

Western Han (206 BC – AD 8)
Length 11.2 cm, weight 568.1g

This crossbow is decorated with gold-and-silver inlaid pattern. On one side of *wangshan* (bow sight) is decorated with peacocks and snake-turtle, and the other side with sparrow, cranes and leopards. Running deer, birds, white tiger biting wild boar are decorated on the other parts of the bow. Along the groove of the arrow shooting is decorated with a very delicate scene of three lively wild geese flying away from a golden arrow behind them. The decoration is similar to that on the crossbow from a princely burial in Sishui, Jiangsu Province (Nanjing 2003:p.19).

Nu, or crossbow, a type of mechanical bow was a long-distant weapon developing from the common bow. A complete *nu* setup would make up of a bronze crossbow device, a wood handle, and a bow. The bronze crossbow is the key part, and is set at the back of the wood handle. Very sophisticated mechanical parts are integrated to make the crossbow more efficient and effective, and at the same time more easy to use.

From archaeological excavations, earlier bronze crossbows were unearthed from the burials M3 and M52 at the old city of Lu State in Qufu, Shandong Province (Shandong 1982:p.154). They were dated to early Warring States period. But these primitive crossbows were set

---

1.南京博物院《泗水王陵考古》第19頁，（香港）王朝文化傳播有限公司2003年版。
2.山東省文物考古研究所等《曲阜魯故城》第154頁，齊魯書社1982年版。

in hollow wooden channels without a bronze holder. During the Han dynasty, bronze holders (*guo*) were commonly used and could provide stronger tension. Incised gradations would appear at the inner side of the bow sight (*wangshan*) for better aiming at the target and making the crossbow more powerful.

展品說明參考書目（英文）

References Cited in the Entries

Anhui 1956
Anhui Sheng Wenwu Guanli Weiyuanhui and Anhui Sheng Bowuguan, *Shouxian Caihou mu chutu yiwu* (Cultural Relics from the Burial of Marquis of Cai in Shhouxian), Beijing: Kexue chubanshe, 1956.

Anyang 1991
Anyang Shi Wenwu Gongzuodui, "Yinxu Qiajiazhuang dong 269 hao mu", *Kaogu xuebao*, 1991.3.

Baoji 2007
Baoji Shi Kaogu Yanjiusuo & Fufengxian Bowuguan, "Shaanxi Fufeng Wujunxicun Xizhou qingtongqi jiaocang fajue jianbao", *Wenwu*, 2007.8.

Baoli 2001
Baoli Yishu Bowuguan, *Baoli cangjin* (Bronzes from the Poly Art Museum), Guangzhou: Lingnan Meishu chubanshe, 2001.

Beijing 1995
Beijing Shi Wenwu Yanjiusuo, *Liulihe Xizhou Yanguo Mudi 1973~1977* (Yan State Cemetery of the Western Zhou Period at Liulihe: 1873-1977), Beijing: Wenwu chubanshe, 1995.

Cao Wei 2006
Cao Wei, *Hanzhong chutu Shangdai qingtongqi* (Shang Bronzes from Hanzhong), Sichuan: Bashu shushe, 2006.

Chang Kuang-yuan 1995
Chang Kuang-yuan, "Chunqiu Jinwengong chenba Zi Fan bianzhong chushi", *The National Palace Museum Monthly of Chinese Art*, 1995.4.

Cheng Changxin 1982
Cheng Changxin et al., "Beijing jianxuan yizu ershibajian Shangdai daiming tongqi", *Wenwu*, 1982.9.

Chen Peifen 2004
Chen Peifen, *Xia Shang Zhou qingtongqi yanjiu* (Studies on the Bronzes of the Xia, Shang and Zhou Periods), 6 vols, Shanghai: Shanghai guji chubanshe, 2004.

Chen Ping 1984
Chen Ping, "Shilun Guanzhong Qinmu qingtong rongqi de fenqi wenti", *Kaogu yu wenwu*, 1984.3 and 1984.4.

Chen Xinren 1980
Chen Xinren, "Suixian Yunyang chutu Chu Zeng Xi qingtongqi", *Jianghan kaogu*, 1980.1.

Chou Fa-kao 1975
Chou Fa-kao (ed.), *Jinwen gulin* (An Etymological Dictionary of Ancient Chinese Bronze Inscriptions), The Chinese University of Hong Kong, 1975.

Cheung Kwong Yue 1997
Cheung Kwong Yue, "Xiangjiang xinjian Caigongzi ji Caihou qi shulue", *Zhongguo wenzi* (Chinese Characters), New vol. 22, Taipei: Yee Wen Publishing Company, 1997.12.

Cheung Kwong Yue 2000
Cheung Kwong Yue, "Xinjian Hu gui mingwen dui jinwen yanjiu de yiyi", *Wenwu*, 2000.6.

Du Jinpeng 1994
Du Jinpeng, "Shang Zhou tongjue yanjiu", *Kaogu xuebao*, 1994.3.

Du Naisong 1964
Du Naisong, "Ji Luoyang Xigong chutu de jijian tongqi", *Wenwu*, 1964.11.

Fang Jianjun 1996
Fang Jianjun, *Zhongguo yinyue wenwu daxi: Shaanxi juan* (A Comprehensive Collection of Chinese Cultural Relics on Music: Shaanxi), Henan: Daxiang chubanshe, 1996.

Fang Jianjun 2007
Fang Jianjun, "Meiguo shoucang de Lai zhong ji xiangguan wenti", *Tianjin yinyue xueyuan xuebao*, 2007.2.

Gansu 1977
Gansu Sheng Bowuguan Wenwudui, "Gansu Lingtai Baicaopo Xizhou mu", *Kaogu xuebao*, 1977.2.

Gansu 1982
Gansu Sheng Bowuguan and Wei Huaiheng, "Gansu Pingliang Miaozhuang de liangzuo Zhanguo mu", *Kaogu yu wenwu*, 1982.5.

Sheng Wenwu Guanlichu, *Mancheng Han mu fajue baogao* (Excavation of the Han Tombs at Man-cheng), Beijing: Wenwu chubanshe, 1980.

Zhongguo 1981
Zhongguo Shehui Kexueyuan Kaogu Yanjiusuo Anyang Gongzuodui. "Anyang Xiaotuncun bei de liang zuo Yin mu", *Kaogu xuebao*, 1981.4.

Zhongguo 1986
Zhongguo Shehui Kexueyuan Kaogu Yanjiusuo, *Yin Zhou jinwen jicheng* (The Collection of Shang and Zhou Inscriptions), vol.4. Beijing: Zhonghua shuju, 1986.

Zhongguo 1988
Zhongguo Shehui Kexueyuan Kaogu Yanjiusuo Anyang Gongzuodui, "1987 nian xia Anyang Guojiazhuang dongnan Yin mu de fajue", *Kaogu*, 1988.10.

Zhongguo 1989
Zhongguo Shehui Kexueyuan Kaogu Yanjiusuo Anyang Gongzuodui, "1986 nian Anyang Dasikongcun nandi de liangzuo Yin mu", *Kaogu*, 1989.7.

Zhongguo 1992
Zhongguo Shehui Kexueyuan Kaogu Yanjiusuo Anyang Gongzuodui, "1980 nian Henan Anyang Dasikongcun M539 fajue jianbao", *Kaogu*, 1992.6.

Zhongguo 1994a
Zhongguo Shehui Kexueyuan Kaogu Yanjiusuo, *Yin Zhou jinwen jicheng* (The Collection of Shang and Zhou Inscriptions), vol.18. Beijing: Zhonghua shuju, 1994.

Zhongguo 1994b
Zhongguo Shehui Kexueyuan Kaogu Yanjiusuo, *Shanxian Dongzhou Qin Han mu* (The Burials of Eastern Zhou, Qin and Han in Shanxian), Beijing: Kexue chubanshe, 1994.

Zhongguo 1998
Zhongguo Shehui Kexueyuan Kaogu Yanjiusuo, *An'yang Yinxu Guojiazhuang Shangdai muzang 1982-1992 nian kaogu fajue baogao* (Guojiazhuang Cemetery of Shang Period within the Yin Ruins, Anyang: Excavations in 1982 - 1992), Beijing: Zhongguo dabaike quanshu chubanshe, 1998.

Zhongguo 2007
Zhongguo Shehui Kexueyuan Kaogu Yanjiusuo, *Yin Zhou jinwen jicheng* (The Collection of Shang and Zhou Inscriptions), revised and enlarged edn., 8 vols, Beijing:

Zhonghua shuju, 2007.

Zhongguo Qingtongqi 1995
Zhongguo Qingtongqi Quanji Bianji Weiyuanhui, *Zhongguo qingtonqi quanji* (A Comprehensive Collection of Chinese Bronzes), vol.8, Beijing: Wenwu chubanshe, 1995.

Zhongguo Qingtongqi 1996
Zhongguo Qingtongqi Quanji Bianji Weiyuanhui, *Zhongguo qingtonqi quanji* (A Comprehensive Collection of Chinese Bronzes), vol.1, Beijing: Wenwu chubanshe, 1996.

Zhongguo Qingtongqi 1997
Zhongguo Qingtongqi Quanji Bianji Weiyuanhui, *Zhongguo qingtonqi quanji* (A Comprehensive Collection of Chinese Bronzes), vol.9, Beijing: Wenwu chubanshe, 1997.

Zhongguo Qingtongqi 1998
Zhongguo Qingtongqi Quanji Bianji Weiyuanhui, *Zhongguo qingtongqi quanji* (A Comprehensive Collection of Chinese Bronzes), vol.4, Beijing: Wenwu chubanshe, 1998.

Zhou Ya 1992
Zhou Ya, "Dantu Jianbi Wangjiashan Dongzhou mu bufen qingtongqi de shidai ji qita", *Shanghai bowuguan jikan* (The Bulletin of the Shanghai Museum), vol.6, Shanghai: Shanghai guji chubanshe, 1992.

Zhou Ya 1997
Zhou Ya, "Shangdai zhongqi qingtongqi shang de niaowen", *Wenwu*. 1997.2.

Zhou Ya 2002
Zhou Ya, "Guanyu Jinhou Su ding jianshu de tantao" (On the Number of the Tripods Ding of Su, Mariquis of Jin) in Shanghai Bowuguan (ed.), *Jinhou Mudi chutu qingtongqi guoji xueshu yantaohui lunwenji* (Proceedings of the Symposium on Bronzes from the Cemetery of Marquis of Jin), Shanghai: Shanghai shuhua chubanshe, 2002.

Zhouyuan 1987
Zhouyuan Fufeng Wenguansuo, "Shaanxi fufeng qiangjia yi hao xizhou mu", *Wenbo*, 1987.4.

Zhu Fenghan 1995
Zhu Fenghan. *Gudai Zhongguo qingtongqi* (Ancient Chinese Bronzes), Tianjin: Nankai daxue chubanshe, 1995.

後 記

初識范季融先生大概是在二十世紀八十年代中期，他當時任職美國萬國商業機器公司（IBM），在同一時候，他爲落實丈人胡惠春先生暫得樓藏瓷捐獻給上海博物館事，往來於美國、上海、香港之間。一九八九年九月，他來到香港中文大學，爲籌劃即將成立的工程學院，出任行政院長（Administrative Dean）兼工程學講座教授。同年十月，《胡惠春、王雲華捐獻瓷器珍品展》在上博開幕。自此至一九九一年六月離港返美，他課餘閑暇常來文物館賜教。范先生給我的印象永遠是溫文儒雅、謙謙君子。這期間，我有更多的機會和他討論文物蒐藏鑒定的共同話題，不時和他一道拜會胡先生，爲暫得樓明清堂名款瓷器請益。范先生在中大爲新學院運籌帷幄，除了奠定各種規範之外，他還向美國太空總署（NASA）和能源部，爲中大爭取了一條接往美國的國際網絡專綫，連接互聯網基幹(backbone)，奠定了中大在互聯網發展的地位，改寫了此後十多年香港學界和全港社會的科技發展。今日，中大仍然肩負管理全港互聯網基幹的任務。飲水思源，如果我們稱范先生爲香港互聯網基幹之父，他當之無愧。

二十世紀九十年代起，上海博物館開始關注海外流散文物市場。期間，范季融先生協助馬承源館長在香港荷李活道文物店，購回西周中期晉國的冒鼎。自此之後，范先生在馬館長的指導下，對青銅器産生了濃厚的興趣，收藏也逐漸有成。

范先生在蒐藏青銅器過程中，可能受到他丈人的收藏理念所影響，他認爲文物藏品應該和庋藏環境配合互補，國寶級的文物不宜私人擁有，這也是普世博物館從業員所恪守的專業規則。守則規定職員在蒐購文物的時候，如有利益衝突，博物館必先有優先權。雖然范先生並非海内外任何一所博物館的職員，在購藏青銅器的時候，他一定將最重要的、最好的先留給上博入藏，必先照顧上博的利益。這也是他的齋名——“首陽齋”的由來。范先生對上博的厚愛不止於此，他和夫人合捐了上博新館的“范季融、胡盈瑩展覽廳”。他們爲多個上博項目提供經費；香港中文大學文物館也多次蒙首陽齋資助活動經費。最近范先生捐贈了明末清初畫家項聖謨的《山水花卉圖册》給上博，册中有郎廷極的引首、跋文、鈐印，爲清初郎窑瓷器的研究提供了寶貴的資料。捐贈也再次體現了范先生所深信的理念，文物最終應該歸得其所，發揮應有的功能和作用。

范先生在文物鑒賞上，尤其是陶瓷器，深受丈人胡惠春先生耳濡目染的影響。但是他在大學和研究院學的是電機工程和物理，科學的基本訓練，加上馬承源館長對他的引導，使他在收藏青銅器的標準、價值、取捨上，與一般銅器藏家有很大的區別，他並沒有純粹以美學角度去鑒賞青銅器。他另辟蹊徑，追求的是另一套的準則。他重視銘文，要以物證史，以器物爲本，去瞭解青銅時代的歷史、文化背景、鑄造業，以及青銅器地域性文化的發展。對范先生而言，青銅器提供了一個很不同的歷史文化視野。這個在上海博物館和香港中文大學文物館兩地展出的展覽，充分體現了范先生的收藏準則和品味。《首陽吉金》展覽的首倡，是蘇芳淑教授在一九九九年向美國華盛頓弗利爾賽克勒美術館提出的。一年後她離美回港，出任中大藝術系講座教授兼系主任，華府展覽建議最終沒有落實。二零零三年十月底，馬承源館長、陳佩芬女士到訪紐約首陽齋，我也敬陪末座，展覽建議重新再上日程。二零零七年上博李朝遠副館長到紐約挑選展品，之後全部展品運返上博，由青銅研究部化驗、清洗、修復、拍照、傳拓、研究、編目。現在展覽卒抵於成，圖錄也及時出版，謹向范先生及上博同人，致以衷心的感謝。

香港中文大學文物館館長

林業強

附表：2008 年後胡盈瑩、范季融捐贈青銅器目錄

《首陽吉金》圖版編號	器名	捐贈對象	備註
2	連珠紋斝	美國芝加哥美術館	
8	獸面紋鬲	美國芝加哥美術館	
14	乳釘雷紋瓿	上海博物館	
18	𦅫冊盤	香港中文大學文物館	
30	晉伯卣	國家文物局	國家文物局撥交上海博物館藏
38	晉侯穌鼎	國家文物局	國家文物局撥交上海博物館藏
40	晉侯對盨	國家文物局	國家文物局撥交上海博物館藏
45	秦公鼎	國家文物局	國家文物局撥交上海博物館藏
46	秦公鼎	國家文物局	國家文物局撥交上海博物館藏
47	秦公鼎	國家文物局	國家文物局撥交上海博物館藏
48	秦公簋	國家文物局	國家文物局撥交上海博物館藏
49	秦公簋	國家文物局	國家文物局撥交上海博物館藏
50	垂鱗紋鎛	國家文物局	國家文物局撥交上海博物館藏
67	商鞅鈹	上海博物館	

AFTERWORD

It must have been in the mid 1980's that I first met Dr. George Fan. He was working at IBM and was commuting frequently between Shanghai, Hong Kong and the States for business and for finalizing the logistics in connection with Mr. J. M. Hu, his father-in-law's wish to donate an important group of ceramics from the Zande Lou collection to the Shanghai Museum. In September 1989, he came to the Chinese University of Hong Kong to serve as Administrative Dean and concurrently Professor in Engineering for the planning of a new Faculty of Engineering in the University. In October in the same year an exhibition of the Zande Lou gift opened at the Shanghai Museum. Within these two years, till June 1991 when Dr. Fan returned to the States, he often came to my office at the Art Museum in his spare time. We exchanged views of common concern on connoisseurship and collecting. George has been a perfect gentleman, always modest about himself and openhearted. Quite a few times he accompanied me to visit his father-in-law for advice on a group of private-hall marked ceramics that the Zande Lou donated to the Art Museum. During this brief stay in Hong Kong, George looked after the inception of the Engineering Faculty, laying down corner stones and devising policies for his followers. He also negotiated with NASA for a connection from Hong Kong to the States, in order to link to the backbone on the internet. Although the connection was effected after George's departure, his proposal and negotiation to the US Government for the link provided a solid foundation for the later vital role of The Chinese University in internet industry and development in Hong Kong. It rewrote the history and laid an important milestone in science and technology in Hong Kong as a whole.

From the early 1990's the Shanghai Museum had begun to pay attention to art and antique objects available for acquisition outside China mainland. Dr. Fan helped Mr. Ma Chengyuan, Director of the Shanghai Museum to salvage from Hong Kong, a mid Western Zhou bronze ding of the Jin State. Mr. Ma introduced Dr. Fan to the world of Chinese bronze and also ignited George's interest in the topic. Before long he formed a very interesting and comprehensive collection. In the course of Dr. Fan's formation of his bronze collection, and probably under the influence of his father-in-law, he has always reckoned that a piece of art or antique should find a proper home. National treasures should never be possessed by a private collector. This is very much in line with universal museum ethics. Museum workers have never been banded from acquiring art and antique objects personally, but if a conflict arises, the rights of the museum should always be given a priority. George has never been a museum staff, yet, in forming his collection he has always put the Shanghai Museum first. The best bronzes and the most important pieces have always been reserved for the Shanghai Museum. He would never touch them. This is also the rationale for coining his private hall name the "Shouyang Studio" (by referring to the anecdote of Bo Yi and Shu Qi of the late Shang). Dr. Fan's dedication to the Shanghai Museum, however, is far beyond this. He and Kitty jointly endowed an exhibition gallery at the Museum, and over the years, have provided funds for many museum programmes and activities. They have also been benefactors and supporters to the Art Museum, The Chinese University of Hong Kong. More recently he donated a landscape and flowers album by the 17th century artist Xiang Shengmo to the Shanghai Museum. The album contains a frontispiece and a colophon by the early Qing imperial porcelain factory supervisor Lang Tingji, and thus, provides useful information for the study and identification of porcelain items attributed formerly to the so-called Lang ware. The gift has witnessed once again, George's life-long belief that important art and antique objects should find a suitable and proper home, so as to manifest their true value and academic significance.

In connoisseurship, Chinese ceramics in particular, George has been following the footsteps of his father-in-law, Mr. J. M. Hu. But he was trained as a scientist and engineer. In his college and postgraduate days he studied electrical engineering and physics. This scientific background, coupled with the personal training and guidance from Mr. Ma Chengyuan, have given him a completely different set of criteria, and priorities in collecting bronzes. He never acquires any piece of bronze merely for its aesthetical value. Instead, he attaches importance to inscriptions – he wants to use his bronzes to reconstruct a fuller picture in the history, culture, technology and provincial development of the Bronze Age in China. To him, Chinese bronzes have provided a very different perspective in history and cultural heritage. The present exhibition, to be open first at the Shanghai Museum, and travel later to the Art Museum, The Chinese University of Hong Kong, reflects Dr. Fan's acquisition policy and personal taste in collecting bronzes. The exhibition was first proposed by Jenny F. So when she was serving at the Freer/Sackler Galleries in Washington D.C. in 1999. Shortly, she returned to Hong Kong to take up a chair-professorship at the Fine Arts Department of the Chinese University. The proposal was, as a result, shelved. In late October 2003, following a visit to the Shouyang Studio in New York by Mr. Ma Chengyuan, Ms. Chen Peifen and myself, the exhibition was put on a schedule again. The selection of the exhibits was performed by Dr. Li Chaoyuan of the Shanghai Museum in New York in 2007. Subsequently the bronzes were shipped to Shanghai for analysis, cleaning, restoration, photography, rubbing, cataloging and study by colleagues at the Bronze Department of the Shanghai Museum. On the occasion of the opening of this exhibition and the publication of an accompanying scholarly catalogue, I should like to express my heartfelt gratitude to George and the Shanghai Museum to make all these possible.

Peter Lam
Director, Art Museum
The Chinese University of Hong Kong

圖書在版編目（CIP）數據

首陽吉金：胡盈瑩、范季融藏中國古代青銅器／首陽
齋，上海博物館，香港中文大學文物館編.－－上海：上
海古籍出版社，2018.11
ISBN 978-7-5325-9002-5

Ⅰ. ①首... Ⅱ. ①首...②上...③香... Ⅲ. ①青
銅器（考古）－中國－圖集 Ⅳ. ①K876.412

中國版本圖書館CIP數據核字（2018）第236586號

責任編輯：吳長青　徐汝聰

裝幀設計：姚偉延　徐莎莎

技術編輯：王建中　陳　昕

首陽吉金
——胡盈瑩、范季融藏中國古代青銅器

首陽齋　上海博物館　香港中文大學文物館　編

上海古籍出版社出版、發行

（上海瑞金二路272號　郵政郵編：200020）
(1) 網址：www.guji.com.cn
(2) E-mail：gujil@guji.com.cn
(3) 易文網網址：www.ewen.co

上海界龍藝術印刷有限公司印刷

開本：635×960毫米 1/8　印張：26
2018年11月第1版　2018年11月第1次印刷
印數：1-1,500
ISBN 978-7-5325-9002-5/K·2563

定價：220.00元